happy home

happy
home

Rebecca Winward

MERRELL
LONDON · NEW YORK

introduction

Ask almost anyone what their dream home looks like, and the chances are they'll describe something large and glamorously decorated, something that sounds as though it has come straight from the pages of a glossy magazine. But does enviable decor alone result in happiness?

Of course, aesthetics are an important part of the interior of a home – they allow us to express our individuality and indulge our tastes – but we should also be aware of the bigger picture. A gorgeous bedspread or an appealing painting will give us a burst of pleasure, but creating a truly happy home requires more than just stylish purchases. By judging a home on its decor alone we make the same mistake as when we judge a book by its cover. A home is a space in which to live and love, to grow up and grow old; it is not simply a pretty backdrop to life, but a practical and integral part of it.

We may be tempted to hinge our happiness at home on the acquisition of expensive furnishings or on whether we are

demonstrating the latest decorating trend, perhaps even on the number of bedrooms our home has, the prestige of its location or the size of its garden. But you have only to consider whether lottery winners or celebrities are truly happier than other folk, and you realize that such materialism isn't the key to happiness. In fact – other than having a loving family and friends around us – what can really make a difference to our well-being and state of mind is to live in an environment that suits all our needs perfectly, and that allows us to indulge in the activities we enjoy.

The effect of domestic architecture on our happiness must not be underestimated. Buildings can evoke a range of emotions. They can make us feel comfortable and safe – snuggled up on a cosy chair by the fire while a gale howls outside, for instance – or they can instil a sense of awe at the beauty of the natural world, for example a stunning view seen through a floor-to-ceiling window. They can also calm a fretful mind by forming a serene and relaxing environment that

opposite
The right decor and furnishings right in a child's room can have a positive impact on their behaviour and happiness.

below
When planning your home, take into account the needs of every member of the family – including pets.

bottom
Comfort is a key consideration in every room, before you even begin to think about style.

Try not to worry about achieving a picture-perfect 'ideal home', and think at first more about function than about form

soothes the senses. They have a greater impact on our mood than many of us realize.

In non-domestic settings, the psychology of design is even used to persuade us to eat more quickly (fast-food restaurants rarely create the sort of ambience to make you want to linger, meaning they can serve more people) or make more purchases (shopping centres are designed to ensure that our gaze falls on the sales messages in shop windows and advertisements). It's powerful stuff. And if these are just the effects that can occur when you are visiting a building, you can imagine the greater influence your home can have, since you're there every day.

It's not just a question of emotion, either, but also one of physical human response. For example, it has been proven that low levels of interior light – perhaps as a consequence of small windows, which are becoming more prevalent in newly built homes – have a direct impact on our being, disrupting our diurnal rhythms and blood-sugar levels, as well as reducing the amount

Each room-by-room chapter contains inspirational pictures of a wealth of gorgeous homes

If you have children, suitable storage for toys and other equipment is even more important.

of vitamin D our bodies can produce, and contributing to depression. The ideal home for health and happiness, therefore, has big windows that let in lots of natural light.

Other architectural factors that can contribute to a positive experience include sizeable rooms (it's well known that cramped conditions are stressful for any living thing), well-proportioned spaces (low ceilings and narrow corridors can feel oppressive) and a good 'flow' from one space to the next (which is part of the reason open-plan living is so popular). Unfortunately, these aspects are, more often than not, present only in expensive, architect-designed properties, rather than in the housing stock as a whole.

In the real world, we can't always trade in our own home for a building that boasts better design, so we must find ways in which to work with what we've got. But no matter the sort of property you start with, there are always ways to improve it and adapt it to your family's needs. So you may not have the luxury of large rooms, or

an endless budget, but that shouldn't be a barrier to creating a happier home. Awkward layouts can be re-engineered, dark or cramped spaces can be opened up using a carefully chosen colour scheme and good lighting, and even levels of natural light can be improved to some extent by the clever use of reflective surfaces.

Try not to worry about achieving a picture-perfect 'ideal home', and think at first more about function than about form. Rather than splashing the cash on a trendy addition with the 'wow' factor, it's far better to invest in well-organized storage systems so that everything has its place (and you can always find what you're looking for), choose finishes and surfaces that are easy to care for and can stand up to the rough and tumble of family life, and plan rooms so that they facilitate easy and enjoyable use.

All this doesn't mean that style shouldn't play a key role: if you've bought this book, then it's likely that you're one of those people for whom a happy home is also a beautiful home. I simply entreat you

to base your decorating decisions on common sense and an awareness of how you and your family wish to use the space. That will result in a far happier home.

This book is your essential guide to achieving that perfect balance of aesthetics and practicality, and you'll discover easy-to-achieve ideas in abundance. Following the first chapter, which explains the basics of creating a happy home, are room-by-room chapters with specific advice for living rooms, dining rooms, kitchens, bathrooms, bedrooms, children's rooms, hallways, home offices and outside spaces. Each contains inspirational pictures of a wealth of gorgeous homes, along with a detailed look at such aspects as layout, colour, furniture and storage. For those short of time (and let's face it, who isn't these days?), the 'happy home hints' suggest quick-fix ideas for instant home happiness, while a 'dos and don'ts' summary provides an at-a-glance guide to the main considerations for the type of room in question.

Happy homemaking!

basics

play

Whether your home is a bijou apartment or a
rambling farmhouse, and whether it's in New
York or England's New Forest, a well-designed
space (in terms of both practical and aesthetic
considerations) will be a happy space. In this
chapter we'll cover the basic principles of
creating a functional, beautiful and ultimately
happier home. Then, in the room-by-room
chapters that follow, you'll find more detailed
advice for each living area.

layout

happy home hint

IF YOU HAVE CHILDREN, DON'T CHOOSE AN INTERIOR STYLE THAT DEMANDS PERFECTION: YOU'LL SPEND ALL YOUR TIME WORRYING ABOUT FINGERPRINTS, DENTS AND SCRATCHES, OR STRAY BITS OF PUREED CARROT. THE LIVED-IN LOOK OF SHABBY CHIC, FOR EXAMPLE, IS MUCH MORE CHILD-FRIENDLY THAN THE HIGHLY POLISHED SURFACES OF ART DECO.

opposite
This arrangement of
rooms allows a beautiful
flow from inside to
outside space.

above
Ensure that furniture
doesn't block the natural
routes through a room,
especially if there is more
than one door.

The optimum layout for home happiness must take various factors into account. There should be enough space for you to fit in all your belongings and still comfortably move around, and there should be a suitable 'flow' between rooms. For example, you wouldn't want to access a bedroom by walking through another bedroom, as the lack of privacy in the latter would make it unfit for purpose; such a space would perhaps be better as a home office, or the two areas could become a master suite, with the smaller one used as a dressing room.

Other common layout niggles include downstairs bathrooms (although that can be mitigated by the addition of a WC upstairs), ground-floor bedrooms (great for elderly relatives, less so for children who aren't keen on bedtime) and properties in which every room is accessed from a narrow corridor (which can feel dark and oppressive). However, whether such floor-plan 'difficulties' are a problem or not will depend on

your personal situation and preferences: again, it's best to think about how you want to use a particular space.

In an ideal world, you'd be able to buy a home that offers the perfect layout, but of course that isn't always possible, either because there is little suitable property in your chosen area, or simply because you have no plans to move. Remember that layouts can be altered: it's easy to swap the functions of more general spaces, such as living rooms, dining rooms and bedrooms, while relocating kitchens and bathrooms, although more time-consuming and expensive, is still absolutely possible. Walls can be removed to open up spaces; even load-bearing ones can be taken out if the appropriate measures are taken, but consult an expert first! If your budget allows, an extension can also provide a solution to layout problems. An architect will be able to advise whether the layout, and not just the square footage of your home, can be improved.

colour

Think about the sort of ambience you'd like to create, and how colour could enhance your sense of well-being. If you lead a busy life, working long days and then entertaining friends or busying yourself with hobbies in the evenings and at weekends, perhaps a calmer ambience is called for, to balance out the hustle and bustle of the everyday. Or you might decide that you need a bright and stimulating space that will help you shrug off the weariness that ensues after a hectic day at the office/shop/school.

Making up a scrapbook of magazine clippings and colour cards, and collecting samples, will help you envisage how your different choices will come together. But you should still always paint test patches – or hang up large samples of wallpaper – before committing to decorating a space, since you'll need to check that the colour looks right *in situ* at different times of day. It is easy to choose slightly the wrong shade (usually one that's a bit darker than you expected), so always gather a selection of samples and make a comparison.

right
The warm tones of this wooden furniture and floor create a cheerful ambience.

below
Knocked-back shades of lime and orange ensure that this interior is colourful but still refined.

walls and floors

The main thing to consider when choosing finishes for walls and floors is ease of cleaning, especially if you have children or pets. Thanks to modern formulations, paint is now available that can be wiped – or even scrubbed – and wallpaper that is tough enough to be cleaned gently. Always select a finish appropriate to the area in which it is to be used; paper, for example, usually isn't the best option for such steamy situations as bathrooms, while a traditional matt paint isn't great for kitchens, since it's easily marked by grease.

Underfoot, you'll want to think not just about ease of cleaning, but also about safety. Areas that can get wet (bathrooms, kitchens, hallways), in particular, should have non-slip flooring. Durability is key. The most heavy-traffic areas should have the most resilient flooring, to withstand high levels of wear and tear; ceramic tiles, good-quality vinyl, timber or a high-quality wool-mix carpet are all excellent choices.

Patterned flooring isn't very fashionable, but it does have the benefit of hiding the inevitable imperfections caused by little 'accidents' (family life and pale cream carpeting aren't really compatible). If you don't like the idea of a pattern as such, opt for a mid-toned carpet with a fleck in it.

above
The use of the same flooring throughout an open-plan space ensures a sense of coherence.

left
If you simply must have wallpaper in the kitchen, clear glass makes an excellent splashback.

furniture

As with many things in life, you should buy the best furnishings you can afford. Upholstered pieces will remain more comfortable for longer, while cabinetry will maintain its good looks. Poor-quality flat-pack is often made from thin chipboard, which doesn't stand the test of time, and easily looks shabby. Solid timber is a far better option, since any damage can be repaired and refinished, or the piece can be given a facelift (if your tastes change, say, or your children want to remodel their rooms as they grow up).

Before buying a new piece of furniture, always make sure it's the right size for its intended spot. It's no good if you find out too late that the new sofa won't fit through the front door, or the super-king bedstead doesn't leave enough room for a wardrobe. It's not just a matter of literal fit, either: consider whether or not the proportions of a piece will suit the space.

Antiques and junk-shop finds can be given a new lease of life with fresh upholstery or a coat of paint.

opposite
Open storage not only
looks decorative, but also
has the benefit of easy
access. You'll have to keep
a duster handy, though.

below
Hiding bits and bobs
in drawers, or behind
cupboard doors, makes
for an uncluttered look.

below, right
When planning storage,
think about the dimensions
of what you need to store, to
make the best use of space.

You can never have too much storage space. 'Divide and conquer' is the best approach, so the most effective solutions will keep like items with like items, maybe even in labelled boxes (depending on what you're storing). A good example of this is hanging shirts together, trousers together, dresses together and skirts together in your wardrobe, but the same principle can be applied to anything from knitting supplies to camera equipment.

Good storage will enable you not only to access items quickly and easily, but also to get the housework done much more speedily, leaving you with more time for doing things you actually enjoy. If everything has its place, it's easier to keep your home tidy, and running a duster or vacuum cleaner around will be a quick job rather than a marathon effort.

soft furnishings

above, left
Rugs, throws, cushions and pouffes will make any room more comfortable.

above
A host of cushions can transform a bed into a sofa – great for a teenager's room.

left
Don't be afraid to have fun with your soft furnishings: they're easily and inexpensively altered if your tastes change.

Even those with an eye for uncompromisingly minimalist design can't pretend that soft furnishings don't have a homely appeal. Cushions, curtains and throws can transform even the most nondescript room, and are the cherry on the cake of a well-designed one.

Whether they are chosen to tone or contrast with the decor, soft furnishings should be made in fabrics that can be kept looking their best, even after washing (preferably) or dry cleaning. Good-quality materials will maintain their looks for far longer than cheap fabrics, so don't be tempted to choose the latter.

lighting

The two main aims of a lighting scheme are to provide comfortable levels of light for the activities being undertaken in each space, and to create the right mood. For both, you'll need a combination of general light sources (perhaps just a pendant hanging in the middle of the ceiling, or inset spots, or wall lights) and directional lighting (such as a reading lamp or special picture lights).

Think about what each room is used for, and what kind of lighting is required where. If you love to curl up in your favourite chair and read a book, for example, a standard lamp positioned just behind it could give just the right illumination. Pay particular attention to task lighting in such areas as the kitchen, where your safety relies on it – when chopping vegetables, for instance.

You don't need to employ a lighting specialist to create different 'schemes' for you (although it's a wonderful option to have); you can simply augment whatever lighting you have already with lamps – either table or standard – and by replacing standard light switches with dimmers. If you choose dimmers, don't forget to buy a compatible type of energy-saving bulb.

Here, three pendant lamps provide an atmospheric option for dining, while inset spots provide illumination for food preparation.

accessories

Decorative pieces are a very personal aspect of our interiors, and a home without artwork of some kind can seem a bit sterile. But don't feel you have to hang pictures everywhere as soon as a room has been decorated, or fill a shelf with knick-knacks immediately after fixing it to the wall. Take time to find pieces that suit your decor and display some individuality.

For example, you could collect family photos or children's drawings, choose several that look great together (odd numbers work best for clusters, and even for more geometric arrangements), frame them and hang them. Or why not try painting your own canvases or sewing a decorative panel? Another great idea is to ask an artist to create something personal that suits your decor and fits the space.

When it comes to ornaments, less is often more. It's far better to have one stunning piece in just the right place than a hoard of smaller ones, which make far less impact visually, and will mean that you'll have to become very well acquainted with a duster. If you have a collection of small curios that you'd like to show off, it's best to house it in a glass-fronted cabinet at a suitable scale for the purpose.

opposite, left
Grouping items of a similar colour together can have a cheerful, decorative effect.

opposite, right
Original artwork adds a personal touch instantly. Try to choose pictures that pick up colours from the room's decor.

at-a-glance guide

DO MAKE SURE THAT YOU CAN MOVE AROUND AND BETWEEN ROOMS COMFORTABLY.

DO PLAN YOUR DECOR BY KEEPING A SCRAPBOOK OF MAGAZINE CLIPPINGS AND COLOUR CARDS, TO HELP YOU ENVISAGE YOUR PERFECT ROOM SCHEME.

DO TEST PAINTS AND WALLPAPER IN SITU.

DO CHOOSE YOUR FLOORING ACCORDING TO THE AMOUNT OF FOOT TRAFFIC THE AREA GETS.

DO CHECK THAT PIECES OF FURNITURE ARE THE RIGHT SIZE FOR THE SPOT YOU HAVE IN MIND – AND THAT THEY WILL FIT THROUGH THE DOOR – BEFORE BUYING THEM.

DO ORGANIZE YOUR STORAGE CAREFULLY, AND REMEMBER THAT YOU CAN NEVER HAVE TOO MUCH.

DO TAKE TIME TO FIND DECORATIVE ACCESSORIES THAT SUIT YOUR DECOR AND HAVE SOME INDIVIDUALITY TO THEM.

DO PLAN YOUR LIGHTING SCHEME AROUND THE ACTIVITIES THAT TAKE PLACE IN EACH ROOM, CONSIDERING THE REQUIREMENT FOR BOTH AMBIENT AND TASK LIGHTING.

DON'T DESPAIR IF THE 'FLOW' BETWEEN ROOMS ISN'T QUITE RIGHT: LAYOUTS CAN BE ALTERED BY REMOVING WALLS OR CHANGING THE FUNCTION OF A ROOM.

DON'T UNDERESTIMATE THE POWERFUL EFFECT COLOUR CAN HAVE ON YOUR MOOD.

DON'T CHOOSE DELICATE, EASILY MARKED FINISHES OR SURFACES IF YOU HAVE CHILDREN OR PETS.

DON'T USE HIGHLY POLISHED FLOOR TILES IN AREAS THAT CAN GET WET. NON-SLIP IS MUCH SAFER.

DON'T SELECT PALE, PLAIN CARPETS UNLESS YOU ARE PREPARED TO HAVE THEM CLEANED REGULARLY.

DON'T BUY POOR-QUALITY FLAT-PACK FURNITURE IF YOU CAN POSSIBLY AVOID IT. SOLID WOOD IS A FAR BETTER INVESTMENT.

DON'T BUY SOFT FURNISHINGS IN CHEAP FABRICS THAT CAN'T BE WASHED (OR, AT THE VERY LEAST, DRY-CLEANED).

DON'T COVER SURFACES WITH ORNAMENTS. LESS IS MOST DEFINITELY MORE IN TERMS OF VISUAL IMPACT AND EASE OF CARE.

living
room

Unless you're lucky enough to have a large house with a separate cinema room, a playroom, a cosy snug and a formal sitting room, your living room will need to multitask to provide a backdrop to all manner of activities. You should first work out what you want to use the area for, then plan your space accordingly – but do be careful not to overcrowd it.

layout

I n any room, it's a good idea to start by working out the position of the largest piece of furniture, and in this space it's likely to be your sofa(s). Many people assume that the best place is against a wall, but that depends on the dimensions of the room. For example, a narrow room can be balanced by placing the sofa at right angles to the long side. This approach is particularly useful if you have an open-plan lounge–diner, and wish to demarcate the living and dining areas.

When arranging seating – whether sofa, chairs or both – remember that the most sociable arrangement is to have them facing, and the least is to line them up next to one another (the 'doctor's waiting room' set-up). It's also a good idea to place

opposite, top
A centrally placed coffee
table is a good option
for a small or medium-
sized room.

opposite, bottom
A pair of sofas – which
don't have to match – work
well when placed opposite
each other.

right
In this cavernous space,
the addition of a partition
wall has helped to define
the different living areas.

a surface of some kind within reach of every seat, complete with coasters, so that drinks can be placed easily to hand.

You'll also want to bear in mind where the television goes in relation to the seating, unless you're lucky enough to have a separate media room. Ideally, everyone should be able to sit where they can see the screen without turning their head. But do be careful not to let the television become the focal point in the room, especially if yours has a big screen. You might want to think about a cabinet, so that the television isn't visible unless it's actually being watched, while die-hard fans could consider building in a projector system with a screen that pulls down from the ceiling, for a cinema-like experience that doesn't take over the space full-time.

Think about other uses of the room, too. Do you read a lot? If so, a comfy chair by the fire (or window), complete with a reading lamp, is a must. Do you have young children? Then incorporate a secure play area, so that you can keep an eye on them while you're chatting with friends or chilling out with a magazine. Are your pets an important part of your family? Creating their own little zone with a big cushion or snuggly blanket allows them to spend time with their human relations in comfort.

left, top
Arranging seating around a fireplace or stove is a cosy option, whether you have a separate living room or an open-plan area.

left
If you watch a lot of films, position your sofa in the best place for the surround-sound system.

colour

right
A variety of whites, beiges and browns creates a natural warmth, but the differing textures ensure that the effect isn't flat.

below
Here, blue and white are used effectively with natural and painted timber for a beach-holiday feel.

I t's likely that you'll spend a lot of time in your living room, so it isn't the place to experiment. Creating a warm and cosy feel (or a cool and comfortable one, in hotter climes) will certainly augment your enjoyment of the room, and will also create the ideal environment for happy days with family and friends. Avoid bright colours unless you're very confident using them, as there is a risk they'll look cheap, and instead think soft, relaxing and sophisticated.

A restricted palette can be a great idea, even if you keep only the floor, walls and large pieces of furniture tone-on-tone together, and then inject contrast with such accessories as cushions, throws and rugs. The best thing about this approach is that you can ring the changes whenever you feel like it.

happy home hint

Loose covers are great for brightening up tired upholstery, protecting pieces from wear and tear, or simply updating the look of your living room. Choose a washable cotton or linen union, but make sure you wash the fabric before making up the covers, so that shrinkage doesn't render them useless. If you're not confident with a sewing machine, find a seamstress to do the job for you, or simply use a big throw and pile on the scatter cushions.

walls and floors

below
Neutral, flat matt walls and a sleek timber floor are complemented by the natural tones and textures of sheepskin, wicker and leather.

below, right
A pale rug on a pale hard floor ensures comfort underfoot without affecting the impression of space.

opposite
Plant-fibre rugs – seagrass, sisal and jute, for example – are great for adding texture and natural warmth.

While a living-room floor doesn't get the same concentrated wear and tear as a hallway, it's still a fairly heavy-traffic area, so make sure you choose your floor-covering accordingly. Carpets should be a hard-wearing wool blend, in a medium shade (possibly with some flecking or mottling), which is much more forgiving than a solid, pale colour. It's inevitable that at some point you'll need to mop up a spill or clean up after someone has traipsed in dirt, so make sure you're aware of the manufacturer's recommendations for spot cleaning (and have suitable cleaning products to hand). It's also a good idea to invest in a stain-repellent treatment when the carpet is new.

Wooden or tiled floors are very durable, and particularly appropriate in a warmer climate, but if you have small children you might want to add a soft rug or two, especially if your little ones are still at the crawling stage. That will also help to lessen any echo effect, which can be a problem (particularly in large spaces) since hard surfaces don't absorb sound. You can also improve the acoustics by using other soft furnishings and upholstery.

Stripped boards have been very popular for a number of years, thanks to the fact that they are an inexpensive option in properties with suspended floors, and have that desirable 'shabby chic' look. As with a solid timber floor (which can be laid over any type of sub-floor), they are hard-wearing, but do make sure that there are no gaps between the boards (re-lay them or use filler if necessary), otherwise the room will be draughty, and you could lose small items in the cracks. Make sure that the boards are sanded very well indeed, for a smooth surface, and that any protruding nails have been knocked below the surface – after all, this type of sub-floor wasn't originally meant to be seen. If you feel the cold easily (or just want to keep your heating bill down), it's worth having a rug at the ready for the winter months, since suspended floors are often lacking in insulation.

Paint is still a wall-decoration favourite, since it's easily redecorated, touched up or cleaned, particularly if a washable formula is used. However, if you have a penchant for wallpaper, the living room is the perfect place to indulge it, since it's less likely to get damaged (as in a hallway), splashed (as in a kitchen or dining room) or drawn on (as in a child's room). It's best to avoid large-scale patterns unless you're lucky enough to have a lot of space – indeed, they can help bring a sense of proportion to a cavernous room – but if you've got a compact home and have fallen in love with a bold paper, why not use it on a feature wall?

With stripped boards and pale-painted walls, this elegant room could be given a fresh new look just by changing the soft furnishings.

furniture

The most important furnishings in this space will be your sofa and/or armchairs, since comfort is imperative. It's worth choosing them not just for their style, but also according to the way you intend to use them. For example, if you like lounging around, then a sofa with an upright back and firm stuffing won't suit you; opt instead for a squishy design with a low back and arms. Tall people should select a model with a deep seat, while shorter people will be more comfortable if the seat is narrower (or they could be left with their legs dangling in order to get support for their back). Low designs are quite popular, as they look sleek and modern, but bear in mind that they can be difficult to get up from, especially for people with limited mobility.

Remember to buy the best you possibly can: your upholstered furniture will get a lot of wear, and cheaper designs simply won't go the distance. The better the piece is made, the more support it will offer, and so it will be more comfortable for longer. However, if you have young children, or a small budget, there's no shame in going for the cheap and cheerful option; just don't expect it to last a lifetime.

Don't bear in mind just the dimensions of your room when choosing sofas and armchairs, but also the width of doorways and any access problems. You don't want to order your perfect upholstered partner only to find that it won't make the hallway turn from front door to living room.

If your home has narrow doorways, or is otherwise awkward when it comes to moving large pieces around, opt for a design with removable arms, or a modular system that can be put together *in situ*. Also remember that furnishings may look smaller in a showroom (many of which are large spaces with high ceilings) than in your own home.

If space is tight, do think about wooden easy chairs (and settees) that have removable cushions, such as the classic Ercol designs. Not only do they take up less space than fully upholstered pieces, but also they have a pleasingly retro vibe, and they're pretty budget-friendly, too. For a more modern look, without splashing more cash, look for the plywood-framed armchairs often stocked by inexpensive furniture stores. For extra-comfortable style on a shoestring, consider popping a loose cover over a single divan, pushing it up against the wall, and piling it high with large cushions.

Finally, it's also a good idea to have some additional seating available for when you have a larger number of guests than usual. Floor cushions, pouffes, folding chairs, stools (which double as low tables) and even dining-room chairs can be pressed into service if the need arises.

left, top
As well as choosing upholstered pieces, have a few occasional chairs that can be used when you have a houseful.

left
Leather sofas and chairs are a hard-wearing choice: many designs look better and better with age.

storage

Think about what you keep in your living room, and plan your storage to accommodate it, allowing a bit of leeway for additional purchases. For example, how many books do you have, and are they mainly small paperbacks or large hardbacks? Heavy books require seriously solid shelving, which could take the form of well-made freestanding bookcases or a heavy-duty wall-hung system. If you have a large library, built-in storage is particularly useful, since it makes use of every inch of space. Books have a decorative quality that many people love, but if you'd rather create a sleeker feel (and not have to dust so much), you could always hide them behind cupboard doors or a sliding panel.

Cleverly chosen occasional tables can also provide storage space, whether you opt for one of the modern purpose-made designs, or simply use an antique chest as a coffee table. They're great for stashing everything from your collection of DVDs to piles of magazines, or even additional blankets and cushions. Alternatively, you could hide any clutter in large storage boxes, which can double as side tables, or in smaller boxes placed on shelves.

previous page
If you're a great reader and have a houseful of books, floor-to-ceiling shelves offer the greatest storage capacity.

left
Unless you have a very modern room and a flashy wall-mounted television, a TV cabinet might be worth considering.

soft furnishings

below
Here, boldly patterned
cushions and throws add
a sense of fun to what is
quite a sober underlying
colour scheme.

right
A throw or blanket not
only adds colour, but also
can be snuggled under on
a cold evening.

With comfort being key, you can't really have too many cushions; then, if you have more guests than usual, someone could sit comfortably on the floor. Throws and blankets are also worth keeping handy, for an easy and cosy solution to chilly evenings that doesn't involve turning up the heating. Make sure that they – and your cushion covers – are machine-washable, so that you can freshen them up if necessary. If you have cats, dogs or small children, it might be best to avoid knitted designs, as pulls are almost inevitable, and they'll quickly look shabby (not in a chic way, either).

You can use soft furnishings to dress your room to suit the season. You'd be surprised at how much the simple addition of a tartan blanket or furry throw can cosy up a leather sofa for winter, or the difference substituting light curtains for heavy ones can make in the summer. You can also introduce a bit of colour to a more restrained room scheme, or try out a slightly new look without the permanence of redecorating.

lighting

As in the case of any space that is used for more than one type of activity, flexibility is key when it comes to lighting the living room. You could have a scheme designed with different modes for specific activities – a low level for relaxation, a brighter option for reading, one that's matched to the brightness of your screen for comfortable television watching – or you could simply have a dimmer switch on the main lighting (whether wall or pendant) and supplement it with well-placed lamps. A standard lamp just behind your favourite chair is good for reading, while uplighters can help to create a soft light that doesn't reflect in the television screen (something to watch out for, particularly if you have wall lights).

below
When positioning intense lighting, such as spots, make sure it can't dazzle anyone sitting in the room.

opposite
Standard lamps are no longer the preserve of traditional interiors: there are some excellent contemporary options available.

accessories

Probably the most personal aspect of any room scheme is the particular collection of accessories, but whatever your preferred style, there are a few rules to follow to ensure maximum impact with minimum effort. It's a better idea to display a few large, carefully chosen pieces than myriad small ornaments, or you may spend more time than you'd like dusting them. In fact, it's worth bearing that in mind when making your choice, since some items are particularly difficult to keep looking spick and span. Dried flowers, for example, are like dust magnets, but usually too fragile to attack with either a cloth or a feather duster.

Family pictures are a great way to add character to the living room, so dig out your photo collection. Why not have some of your favourite shots framed, or even printed as canvases? If you feel like splashing out and having some truly unique artwork on your walls, you could find a local artist whose style you admire, and ask them to create some family portraits.

Not only are houseplants attractive, but also they're a healthy addition, since they can have a purifying effect on the air. Shrivelled and yellowing plants do nothing to improve the ambience of a room, however, so have them only if you can keep them looking their best, and choose them according to how green your fingers are. If you're not fond of the idea of regular houseplant maintenance, a simple vase of flowers adds an instant 'dressed' touch.

happy home hint

RAID THE FAMILY PHOTO ALBUM FOR NOSTALGIC SHOTS, AND HANG COLLECTIONS OF THEM TOGETHER, USING THE SAME STYLE OF FRAME TO ENSURE COHERENCE. IF YOU WANT TO INTRODUCE EVEN MORE UNITY, SCAN THE PICTURES INTO YOUR PC AND PRINT BLACK-AND-WHITE VERSIONS FOR A VINTAGE-STYLE DISPLAY.

below
Mixing books, magazines, family photos and ornaments means that handy storage doubles as a decorative feature.

opposite, top
The sleek shape, bold colouring and shiny finish of this collection of vases echo not only the lamp alongside, but also other elements of the decor.

opposite, bottom
Here, white shelves on a white-painted wall provide a neutral backdrop for an eclectic collection of objects.

at-a-glance guide

DO ARRANGE SEATING SO THAT PEOPLE CAN FACE ONE ANOTHER WHEN SITTING DOWN.

DO PLACE A COFFEE TABLE OR SIDE TABLE WITHIN EASY REACH OF EVERY SEAT.

DO CHOOSE YOUR SOFA FOR COMFORT AS WELL AS STYLE.

DO BUY THE BEST-QUALITY FURNISHINGS YOU CAN AFFORD.

DO MAKE EXTRA SEATING PROVISION FOR WHEN YOU HAVE A HOUSEFUL.

DO CREATE A SOPHISTICATED AND RELAXING AMBIENCE: UNLESS YOU'RE CONFIDENT WITH COLOUR, BOLD SHADES ARE BEST RESTRICTED TO ACCESSORIES.

DO SELECT A HIGH-QUALITY FLOORCOVERING THAT WILL COPE WITH THE INEVITABLE WEAR AND TEAR.

DO ACCESSORIZE A HARD FLOOR WITH A SOFT RUG OR TWO.

DO CHOOSE YOUR BOOKSHELVES ACCORDING TO THE SIZE (AND WEIGHT) OF YOUR BOOK COLLECTION.

DO CONSIDER USING A CHEST OR BOX AS A COFFEE TABLE, SINCE THE STORAGE SPACE INSIDE IS INVALUABLE.

DO CREATE A FLEXIBLE LIGHTING SCHEME.

DO PERSONALIZE THE SPACE WITH FAMILY PHOTOS OR ORIGINAL ARTWORK.

DON'T ASSUME YOUR SOFA MUST BE POSITIONED WITH ITS BACK TO THE WALL.

DON'T OVERCROWD THE SPACE WITH TOO MANY PIECES, OR WITH FURNITURE THAT'S TOO LARGE.

DON'T BUY A SOFA WITHOUT CHECKING THAT IT WILL FIT THROUGH THE FRONT DOOR, ALONG THE HALL AND INTO THE LIVING ROOM.

DON'T POSITION SEATING SO THAT PEOPLE CAN'T SEE THE TELEVISION WITHOUT TURNING THEIR HEADS.

DON'T LET THE TELEVISION DOMINATE THE ROOM. IT'S A GOOD IDEA TO BUY A CABINET TO HIDE IT AWAY WHEN IT'S NOT IN USE.

DON'T OPT FOR A LIGHT-COLOURED CARPET: A MID-TONE IS BEST, ESPECIALLY IF IT HAS A DARKER FLECK IN IT.

DON'T FORGET TO MAKE SURE THAT THERE ARE NO LARGE GAPS BETWEEN STRIPPED FLOORBOARDS.

DON'T OVERPOWER A SMALL ROOM WITH A LARGE-SCALE PATTERNED WALLPAPER; OPT FOR A SMALLER MOTIF OR MAKE A FEATURE WALL.

DON'T BE TEMPTED TO SKIMP ON CUSHIONS AND THROWS.

DON'T CHOOSE DELICATE SOFT FURNISHINGS THAT CAN'T BE WASHED. FABRICS THAT CAN BE DRY-CLEANED ARE FINE, BUT NOT QUITE AS CONVENIENT AS MACHINE-WASHABLE ONES.

DON'T HAVE HOUSEPLANTS IF YOU'RE NOT SURE YOU CAN KEEP THEM LOOKING THEIR BEST.

DON'T CHOOSE ORNAMENTS THAT MAKE HOUSEWORK LABORIOUS.

dining room

Whether yours is a separate, formal dining room or a more casual, open-plan eating area, it's a very important part of the home; after all, sitting down with family and friends to share a meal is one of life's great pleasures. If you get this space right, friends will not only be more likely to accept an invitation, but also linger longer when they do.

layout

Although we might all sneak a meal while watching our favourite drama series every now and again, eating on your lap in front of the television is less than sociable, so it's well worth finding space for a dining table and chairs, even if it's just a small one. As long as you have 90 centimetres between the table and the nearest wall, you can fit a dining area into a relatively compact space. However, if the measurement is between the table and a piece of furniture with doors or drawers, it should be increased to allow easy access to the storage.

Whether you wish to create a formal or an informal space, proximity to the kitchen is crucial: no one wants to have to carry hot dishes far to reach the table. But other than that, there is relative flexibility in where you site your dining area, and in homes worldwide you will see dining tables placed in kitchens, conservatories, spacious hallways and areas open-plan to living rooms or kitchens, as well as in dedicated, separate dining rooms.

Depending on the layout of your home, your dining area might also need to act as a thoroughfare. If so, make sure you position the table so that you don't have to alter your line too much to avoid it (one day you'll take a straighter route than you should have, and could walk right into it).

opposite
Thanks to its castors, this chunky dining table can easily be moved if required.

left, top
This long, narrow table has been chosen to suit its long, narrow location, to make sure there's a comfortable space around it.

left
By being lined up with the window, this table is 'anchored' in the open-plan space.

colour

below
In a room of largely neutral tones, the red of the paintings and the single chair adds a quirky vibrancy.

below, right
The dining room can double as a library, and you can maximize the decorative potential of your collection by ordering it by colour.

In this space, the modern approach is to create a light, bright feel; dark colours are generally considered a bit old-fashioned, although when used with panache they can break away from the historical cliché. If you're not confident with colour, it's best to take the former approach, but given the nature of the dining room, a bold and theatrical treatment can have great impact. A word of warning, though: if your room is open-plan, you'll need to ensure that your scheme for the dining area flows through to the adjoining space, too.

Proportions should also be borne in mind when selecting your colour scheme. Large rooms can take strong colours, but that doesn't necessarily mean you should use them – pale can be interesting. In a small room, try using a restricted palette and keeping decoration minimal for extra impact.

walls and floors

While the dining room doesn't need as much consideration as other rooms when it comes to selecting a paint formula or wallpaper type (it doesn't have the airborne moisture found in the kitchen, for example), you might want to choose a washable paint if you have small children: if they can get pureed carrot in their hair, they can certainly get it on your walls. But even if you don't have that concern, you might want to avoid delicate paint finishes in such places as behind a sideboard or around a serving hatch, or your beautiful matt paint might be damaged by splashes and spillages.

Similarly, a washable floor surface is best, because accidents do happen (and you don't want guests to feel awful because they've stained your shag-pile with a dropped glass of Rioja). Timber has an inherent natural warmth and beauty, while tiles can be a very affordable and practical solution. If you choose the latter, you might want to consider Spanish skirting, which gives the impression of more space by extending the 'floor surface' slightly up the walls.

If you like the tactile nature of carpet, go ahead, but make sure you also put a large, inexpensive rug beneath the table, either to tone in with the carpet or to contrast. If it gets stained beyond cleaning, it can always be replaced.

previous page
Here, the tongue-and-groove panelling on the walls is echoed by the similarly coloured timber floorboards.

left, top
A washable floor is a sensible option in any dining room, not just in a sleek, contemporary one.

left
A practical timber floor has been used throughout this open-plan room, with a rug to demarcate the living area.

50

dining room

furniture

left
Don't feel constrained by what a piece 'should' be used for. Here, a wardrobe has been used in a dining area, to great effect.

below
Small tables are great for compact rooms or informal eating areas, but if you like entertaining, you should try to make space for a larger example.

I f you haven't much room, investigate space-saving options. Gateleg tables can be folded down to occupy a small footprint when not in use, and there are also extending designs with sliding leaves, or those where sections can be inserted into the middle of the tabletop. Folding or stacking chairs can also help, or you could simply use your dining chairs in other parts of the house – say at an occasional desk or by your bed – and fetch them whenever they are required for dining.

Round tables are considered most sociable, since everyone is seated facing one another, while a pedestal base ensures that nobody sits uncomfortably close to a table leg. However, non-extending square or rectangular tables are fine with a leg at each corner, and you should always choose the right shape of table for the space available.

Tabletops are often made of wood (perhaps with a veneer), but there is a modern trend for glass. This can help to evoke a sense of space, owing to its transparency, but remember that it (and any other highly polished surface, for that matter) will show every smear and scratch.

You'll also want to consider the relative heights of your table and chairs. Is there room for your thighs to tuck in comfortably beneath the table? It's especially important to check this if you don't buy your dining chairs as a set. What's known as a

'harlequin' set of mismatched dining chairs can look great, but you need to make sure that they're all roughly the same height and proportion. You can ensure coherence by choosing a variety of different designs in similar materials, shapes or colours.

Comfort is of great importance, especially if your vision is of family and friends spending many happy hours around the table, sharing food, memories and ideas. Chairs with hard seats may be easy to clean – and look sharp and modern – but can seem a little hard on the buttocks after a while (especially stools, or benches that don't offer back support), so either cushions or upholstered seats may be called for. If you choose the latter, make sure you avoid expensive fabrics or those that can't be spot-cleaned with water. If you're still worried about spillages, you could treat the fabric with a stain repellent, or make use of washable loose covers.

opposite, top
If you love the retro look, you'll be spoilt for choice when it comes to selecting that dining-room staple, the sideboard.

opposite, bottom
Seating doesn't have to match to be stylish, but try to make sure that your harlequin set has common proportions and some coherence in terms of design.

right
A glass table with clear acrylic chairs makes for an ethereal look when placed in a white room.

storage

Because an extra surface close to the table for wine, water, condiments and serving dishes is always handy, the traditional options of sideboard or dresser are a good choice in this space. All sorts of fresh takes on these pieces are available, so you don't have to take the idea of 'traditional' too seriously. Contemporary makers have created some beautiful options, while fantastic vintage finds from the middle of the twentieth century can be bought from online auctions and specialist dealers. But don't feel confined to these conventional storage options: shelves, console tables, chests of drawers or even industrial-style trolleys can do perfectly well.

below, left
Here, an eclectic collection of china works well thanks to the white-on-white effect ...

below
... while this riotous collection of platters is given added zing by being displayed on a lime-green dresser.

Such items as heatproof mats, tablecloths, napkins and candles should be stored in the dining area, for easy access. It's best not to keep everyday crockery here – unless your dining space is right next to the kitchen – but if you have attractive china that is used less often, you might want to put it on open shelves as decoration, bearing in mind that it'll need to be dusted periodically, and probably washed before use. Just don't store plates and bowls in tall stacks, because it increases the chance of chips and cracks if you try to take one out from the middle. Also, don't put glasses upside down: it weakens the rim and makes them vulnerable to chipping, and they can even break under their own weight.

above
A sleek sideboard is the contemporary version of the dresser, and is ideal for storing tableware, glassware and linens.

right
A traditional dresser provides lots of storage, and is worth considering if you have the space.

happy home hint

YOU MAY ALREADY HAVE TWO SETS OF CHINA, GLASSWARE, LINEN OR CUTLERY, BUT SAVING ONE FOR 'BEST' COULD BE A LITTLE POINTLESS - YOU MAY FIND IT NEVER GETS USED.

soft furnishings

right
A wipe-clean tablecloth is a great idea for everyday dining, and a huge variety of patterns and plains is available.

right, bottom
Sitting on folding chairs can be a bit uncomfortable for long periods, but it's nothing a squishy cushion can't fix.

Table linen can make the scruffiest table look stylish. It doesn't have to be expensive: vintage white bedsheets are great, because they are of the sort of quality that isn't easily affordable these days; or you could make your own tablecloth from cheap lengths of cotton (your local fabric shop is likely to have all sorts of options, including florals, ginghams, spots, stripes and plains). Just make sure that the fabric you choose is machine-washable.

Whatever type of cloth you use, always add a table-saver, which is waterproof on one side and felted on the other. It will protect the surface beneath not only from liquid spills, but also from damage from sharp objects and, to some extent, heat. It is a good idea to have napkins to hand, and the bigger the better; they're not only for dabbing mouths and wiping fingers, but also the first line of defence if a spill occurs (since speedy action helps to prevent staining). For informal meals, break out your stash of paper napkins, but you might want to invest in a set of fabric ones for special occasions.

happy home hint

PVC-COVERED COTTON IS GREAT FOR PROTECTING TABLETOPS, ESPECIALLY IF YOU'RE EXPECTING SPILLS, FROM EITHER SLIGHTLY CARELESS DINERS OR SMALL CHILDREN. DON'T FORGET TO USE HEATPROOF MATS FOR HOT DISHES, THOUGH.

dining room

lighting

A gorgeous antique chandelier takes pride of place over the dining table in this elegant room.

The key to lighting a dining area is to get the levels right: too low, and your diners won't be able to see what they're eating; too high, and any chance of feeling comfortable and relaxed is lost. With that in mind, if you have a single pendant fitting, a dimmer switch is essential, while a multi-option lighting scheme is nice to have. If you have an open-plan kitchen–diner, though, you must have separate switches for the lights in these areas, so that you can flick a switch and plunge the kitchen into darkness during the meal (hiding the post-cookery mess from your diners).

A pendant fitting hung low above the centre of the table not only provides a useful pool of light in just the right place, but also has a certain balanced aesthetic. Rise-and-fall designs are flexible, or there are single- or multi-pendant fittings to suit the shape of many tables and various styles. Wall lighting with lower wattage bulbs can create a cosier ambience (certainly, don't choose bulbs that create a cool white light), while on a special occasion, candles on the table will add an atmospheric touch.

accessories

right
In this open-plan living/
dining room, the cheerful
colours of the tablecloth
pick up the brights in the
cushions, giving the whole
space coherence.

below
Here, the use of red
gingham for both the seat
cushions and the napkins is
a nice decorative touch.

opposite, top
The little boxes on chapel
chairs were made for hymn
books, but are also great
for napkins and cutlery.

If you want to trade in tired and worn crockery, try to choose a design that will complement the decor in your dining room. There's no rule that says you have to buy a matching set, and it can be more fun (and more visually interesting) to collect individual pieces from junk shops, charity shops, markets or auctions. Alternatively, choose pure-white china in classic shapes. Most shops do a range, and you can mix and match brands until you get the sort of collection you're looking for. Do, however, try to find pieces of the same weight, so that the mismatched 'set' has some coherence. Catering supply outlets are a great source of white tableware, particularly if you're on a tight budget.

As well as being a fine spot to display your crockery, the dining room could prove the perfect backdrop for other collections, too. Whether you have a cabinet full of vintage glassware, or hang the walls with a selection of artwork or family pictures, you're sure to provide a talking point at mealtimes, as well as adding a decorative touch.

at-a-glance guide

DO FIND A SPOT FOR A DINING TABLE AND CHAIRS, EVEN IF IT'S JUST A SMALL ONE.

DO CHOOSE YOUR COLOURS ACCORDING TO THE PROPORTIONS OF THE ROOM AND ITS RELATIONSHIP TO OTHER SPACES.

DO THINK ABOUT WHETHER YOU NEED WASHABLE FINISHES ON WALLS AND FLOORS.

DO LOOK OUT FOR INNOVATIVE TABLE DESIGNS AND STACKING OR FOLDING CHAIRS, IF SPACE IS TIGHT.

DO BUY A TABLE TO SUIT THE SHAPE OF YOUR ROOM.

DO CONSIDER COLLECTING A STYLISHLY MISMATCHED SET OF DINING CHAIRS.

DO MAKE SURE YOUR TABLES AND CHAIRS HAVE A COMFORTABLE DIFFERENCE IN HEIGHT.

DO CHOOSE UPHOLSTERED SEATING, FOR EXTRA COMFORT.

DO SELECT STORAGE THAT CAN BE HOME TO WINE, WATER AND CONDIMENTS DURING MEALS.

DO KEEP TABLE LINEN, MATS, CANDLES AND OCCASIONAL CROCKERY IN A PLACE THAT'S ACCESSIBLE EVEN IF EVERY SEAT AROUND THE TABLE IS FILLED.

DO THINK ABOUT HOW TO CREATE THE PERFECT LIGHT LEVELS FOR MEALTIMES.

DON'T PLACE YOUR DINING TABLE TOO CLOSE TO THE WALL, OR TO ANOTHER PIECE OF FURNITURE.

DON'T FORGET THAT A DINING TABLE CAN ALSO BE USED AS A DESK AND A PLAY AREA.

DON'T SITE YOUR DINING AREA TOO FAR AWAY FROM THE KITCHEN.

DON'T CHOOSE A LIGHT-COLOURED CARPET WITHOUT PROTECTING IT WITH AN INEXPENSIVE RUG.

DON'T CHOOSE A HIGHLY POLISHED TABLETOP: IT WILL SHOW EVERY FINGERPRINT OR TINY SCRATCH.

DON'T EXPECT GUESTS TO SIT ON BENCHES FOR ANY MEAL WITH MORE THAN TWO COURSES.

DON'T STACK PLATES HIGH, OR STORE GLASSES UPSIDE DOWN – THEY COULD GET DAMAGED.

DON'T FEEL LIMITED TO 'DINING-ROOM FURNITURE'. IF A PIECE WORKS IN THE SPACE, USE IT.

DON'T WORRY ABOUT THAT SCRUFFY TABLE: SMARTEN IT UP WITH A TABLECLOTH.

DON'T FORGET TO PROVIDE NAPKINS FOR THE DINERS' CONVENIENCE (AND AS A QUICK SPILL-LIMITING DEVICE).

DON'T INVEST IN 'BEST' CHINA, GLASSWARE, LINENS OR CUTLERY: THEY MAY NEVER GET USED.

kitchen

You've probably heard it said that the kitchen is the heart of the home. It may be a cliché, but that's because it's true. Most modern kitchens witness a combination of cookery, laundry, dining and work (whether school or salaried), so, with such a lot of different needs to be fulfilled, it's crucial to get this room right.

layout

The first thing to consider is the layout of your kitchen. The two most important areas to have close links with the kitchen are the dining and living rooms: the former for obvious reasons (nobody wants to have to carry dishes any distance to the table), the latter so that the cook does not feel isolated while preparing food, whether for an everyday family meal, or for a group of guests on a special occasion. It's pretty miserable being the one stuck on your own, doing the cooking, while everyone else is being sociable.

If your home doesn't have this convenient layout, consider whether you might switch the

This layout – an open-plan kitchen with a comfortable seating area that opens out on to the garden – is great for modern lifestyles.

right
If there's room in your kitchen for an informal dining area, do take that opportunity.

below
'Living kitchens' allow a family to spend more time together, and nobody is left out simply because they have to go and cook.

below, right
An L-shaped room doesn't have to be awkward; it's just a case of choosing the right layout and furnishings.

functions of various spaces, or find out whether it's possible to knock through into an adjoining room, to create either an additional doorway or a more open-plan space. If you like the idea of open-plan but don't want the hassle or expense of getting the builders in, you could try simply removing an internal door or two to create the illusion of more space.

Make sure your kitchen is laid out using the idea of a 'working triangle'. This configuration of food storage, cooking and preparation areas is designed to minimize the number of steps required to prepare a meal. The good news is that many modern homes will already have a kitchen that adheres to this principle, but if yours doesn't for some reason, consider where changes could be made to improve the situation.

kitchen
colour

right
Here, the metallic patina of the tabletop and the rich tones of the chairs and table legs add gravitas to a pale colour scheme.

below
Great for the vintage look, a scheme of pale green and cream can be livened up with punctuations of pillar-box red and mid-blue.

above
In this room, the only touches of colour come from the storage boxes, yet the whole space appears cheerful and bright.

Nowhere is the right colour scheme more important than in the kitchen, since the investment is greater and, for the most part, more permanent than in other parts of the house. In addition, if yours is a 'living kitchen' rather than just a food-preparation area, it's a room in which you'll be spending a lot of time.

It's a good idea to look in magazines and online for inspiration, but try not to get too hung up on the latest trends. Instead, select a scheme you know you'll like for a very long time. Not only are replacement units and surfaces expensive, but also remodelling causes inconvenience by taking a much-used room out of action for a while.

With that in mind, it's worth choosing classic cupboard doors, worktops and tiles, so they stand the test of time. If you're tempted by a strong colour, ask yourself whether you'll still love it in five years' time. If in any doubt, choose a neutral shade instead, and use your favourite vibrant shade of paint on the walls, or opt for bright accessories. Paint and accessories are more easily switched should you find the appeal of your chosen scheme waning after a few years.

left
White goods don't come only in white these days: there are many colourful options available.

below, left
Just one wall painted with a strong shade can create a dramatic effect – and it's easily repainted if you change your mind.

below
This vibrant turquoise is the perfect foil for the red colander and plastic canister, and the grass-green of the two mugs.

walls and floors

above
Ceramic tiles are a no-nonsense option for walls and floors, and they won't break the bank.

right
Marble (or even marble-effect) tiles can give your kitchen that grand country-house feel.

opposite
Get out the blackboard paint, and you have the perfect place to leave little notes and write down shopping lists.

The main thing about kitchen surfaces is that they should be durable and easy to clean. Practical floor options include ceramic tiles, which have the benefit of being suitable for a wide range of budgets as well as hard-wearing and easy to clean, and floor-coverings including vinyl and rubber, which have similar attributes but are kinder on dropped crockery. The latter are also free of joints or grout-lines, as long as they're in sheet rather than tile form, making for even easier cleaning – although not everyone is fond of their aesthetics. If your budget is rock-bottom low, try painting the concrete sub-floor (if there is one) with floor paint to brighten it up and help to prevent staining.

If your budget is rather grander, there are myriad beautiful options out there, but try not to get carried away and forget the practicalities of family life. Natural stone might be beautiful, but, before you take the plunge, consider that it does require more maintenance. Stone is porous, and can stain if not properly sealed, and it needs re-treating periodically, too.

When it comes to walls, many kitchens are largely painted, with splashbacks between wall and floor units to make cleaning easier. Whatever the colour, make sure the paint you choose is specially designed to cope with the inevitable grease and condensation, as this type of formula will also be washable.

Your main concern when choosing splashback material is also ease of cleaning: a washable surface is crucial. Ceramic tiles look great and are available in a wide range of styles and price brackets, but do think about the grout. White grout can discolour with time, and can stain, so make sure you use a high-quality product that features protection against mould, and consider using a sealant over

the top. Or why not use a coloured grout? Cream or grey might prove a more practical choice than white, and can look fantastic: white or cream metro-style tiles look brilliantly retro with grey grout lines, for example.

Alternatively, a variety of sheet materials will fit the bill nicely. For industrial chic, stainless steel looks smart (although you must be careful not to use an abrasive cleaner, as it will scratch), while back-painted glass is available in a huge range of colours and gives a wonderfully crisp modern look – and it couldn't be easier to clean.

left
Back-painted glass splashbacks are superbly easy to clean, and come in any colour you could want.

below
Stripped boards look as good in the kitchen as in any other room, and just seem to get better with wear and tear.

furniture

Whether you opt for freestanding or fitted furniture, take the long-term view and buy the best you can afford. You won't regret your decision, since years down the line your lovely kitchen will have stood the test of time.

Fitted units have the benefit of using every inch of available space, but freestanding pieces can be moved around if required (although you will need to clean under and behind them regularly). When buying fitted units, don't be persuaded to purchase such expensive 'space saving' storage as pull-out larders and 'magic' corners unless they're easy to clean (food can fall through the wire framework and be difficult to get to without dismantling things), or unless you're so desperately in need of space that it's worth the trade-off.

Choosing the right finish is also important. Vinyl and foil-wrapped doors are budget-friendly and easily wipeable, but you can't beat natural timber for its warmth and beauty. As long as the wood is given a coat of some kind of sealant, cleaning won't be a problem. Painted doors should also boast a protective finish, and a big bonus is that, should they start to look tired and shabby, they can be given a new lease of life with a fresh coat of paint.

As far as worktops go, standard laminate is often the best choice, because it's maintenance-free and durable, as well as inexpensive. More pricey options, such as timber and granite, are beautiful but can be damaged more easily: lemon juice can

above
Freestanding furniture gives you the benefit of being able to change its layout easily, and you can take it with you when you move house.

left
An island unit on castors is a great idea for a small, busy kitchen.

corrode stone, for example, and wood can become stained if it isn't well sealed. If you choose a wooden worktop, opt for an oiled finish, as you can sand and touch up any problem areas without having to refinish the entire run. Don't forget, whichever worktop type you have, you'll always need to keep chopping boards and trivets near preparation surfaces.

If you have space, a washable kitchen table can be a very valuable addition, since it doubles as a preparation surface; more delicate tabletops can be protected with an oilcloth cover. This useful piece of furniture can also function as a desk if you work from home, and is also handy if you want to keep an eye on the kids doing their homework while you cook dinner. If you haven't room for a full-size table, why not consider a small fold-down version attached to the wall? In addition, folding stools that can be hung on the wall when not in use are a great space-saving solution.

Shaker style is timeless, and particularly suitable for introducing a slightly more clean-lined feel in a period property.

happy home hint

HOWEVER MUCH CUPBOARD SPACE YOU HAVE IN A KITCHEN, IT NEVER QUITE SEEMS ENOUGH. ONE OF THE REASONS CAN BE THAT ALL SORTS OF 'STUFF' HAS BEEN ACCUMULATED OVER THE YEARS, SO A PROPER CLEAR-OUT COULD REALLY HELP TO MAKE YOUR EXISTING STORAGE MORE WORKABLE. TAKE A TRIP TO THE CHARITY SHOP WITH THE UNNECESSARY ITEMS THAT HAVE BEEN TAKING UP SPACE IN YOUR KITCHEN, AND NOT ONLY WILL YOU FEEL HAPPIER, BUT ALSO SOMEONE ELSE WILL.

kitchen
storage

left
Keep things near to where they're likely to be used; for example, seasonings and spices close to the hob.

below
There are all sorts of imaginative storage options that are attractive as well as practical, although some can be expensive.

opposite
This great *batterie de cuisine* offers pan storage galore, and ensures they're close to hand when needed.

In a room with so many functions, it's hardly surprising that one of the most common complaints is a lack of suitable storage. Not only is this frustrating, because it takes so much more time and effort to find what you're looking for, but also clutter means that cleaning takes longer.

However, there are a variety of ways in which you can maximize your storage, even if you're not planning a major refit. For example, take a look in your cupboards and check the height between shelves compared with the height of the items stored there. You may well find a big gap that exists purely so you can find what you're looking for. Try packing foodstuffs, or even infrequently used crockery and gadgets, into plastic storage boxes that can be placed on shelves that are much closer together, and pulled out for the required item to be selected. The majority of off-the-shelf kitchen cupboards will already have inside them the holes for adjusting shelf positions, so it's just a case of buying additional shelves and fixings from a kitchen retailer or DIY store.

Wall- and ceiling-mounted solutions are exceedingly useful, as they take up no worktop space and avoid the need to rummage in a

happy home hint

For instantly improved pan storage, fix a hanging rack above the sink, making sure that it's securely fastened to the ceiling joists. This is the most efficient way of storing these kitchen essentials, as their handles and lids can take up a surprising amount of cupboard space; they'll also be close at hand when you want to use them. If you can, choose pans with lids that will hook over the handle when they're hung on the rack.

cupboard or drawer. As well as standard open shelves, there are designs with hanging hooks, plate racks and spice drawers, and even splashback-mounted storage systems. A good low-budget option is to fix a rail underneath a wall shelf, and hang things on butchers' hooks. Everyday utensils can be placed in a jug by the hob so they're readily accessible. However, do remember that open storage can be susceptible to a build-up of dust and grease. It's best to use it only for everyday items that you want close to hand, and be prepared to give everything a periodic wash. Alternatively, you could invest in a set of smart wipeable storage boxes to put on the shelves.

Also think carefully about how much storage you'll need for fresh food. There's little more frustrating than realizing your fridge doesn't have the capacity you need, and you could waste food, too, if there isn't room for leftovers (which, being a very fast supper option, can be a godsend on particularly busy days). Worse still, finding you've reached critical mass refrigeration-wise in the run-up to a special occasion can add stress to the otherwise enjoyable preparation.

opposite
Open storage is great for small, country-style kitchens, but you will find that less regularly used items will need cleaning periodically.

left
Floor-to-ceiling units use every inch of space available, and also have the benefit of a sleek, uncluttered appearance.

soft furnishings

right
This pretty cushion picks up the duck-egg blue from the dining area, and injects extra warmth with its pink tones.

below
Curtains are in keeping with the cottage look, but remember to choose a washable fabric so that cooking smells can be easily removed.

For ease of cleaning, consider whether you really need soft furnishings in the kitchen. Windows that aren't overlooked, for example, might be best left undressed, while those that can be peered through from outside might be suited to a wipeable Venetian blind. If you do hanker after curtains, or have the sort of living kitchen that features a window seat or sofa, then choose washable fabric (and loose covers, in the case of the seating).

If your kitchen is open-plan to a living room, there will of course be upholstered furniture, cushions and maybe curtains in the same space; you want it to be cosy and comfortable, after all. But there is a way to ensure that smells, grease and airborne residue don't permeate the fabrics in this part of your home: a top-notch extraction system, which will vent the stale air to the outside.

kitchen
lighting

right
Here, a big industrial-style lamp has been used as an imaginative take on task lighting, positioned above the hob.

right, bottom
If your kitchen has a dining area, a low-slung pendant over the table is a stylish option.

Make the most of any natural light by ensuring that window dressings, if you have them, don't limit the amount coming into the room – inset Roman blinds are particular culprits here – and by using pale shades to help bounce the light around. If your windows are on the small side, you could also try replacing solid internal doors with glazed ones, to 'borrow' light from other spaces.

A good lighting scheme can make a huge difference to any room, but in a kitchen, with its many different functions, it's critical. You'll need both task and ambient lighting, and if your space is open-plan, the latter is all the more important: you should be able to turn lights on in a variety of combinations for different 'moods'.

Well-positioned task lighting will ensure that you can prepare food on the surfaces without

above
Glass splashbacks can be backlit, using strips of LEDs, for a dramatic effect.

left
The addition of a rooflight has made all the difference in this tiny kitchen.

opposite
This kitchen benefits from inset spots for ambient lighting, and stylish contemporary pendants to highlight the island unit and provide task lighting.

working in your own shadow. This can be achieved by inset spots in the ceiling, just in front of the wall cabinets, and also by under-cabinet lighting (often operated from a separate switch). Ceiling spots can also provide ambient light; they are a great option since they're unobtrusive, and modern LED versions are energy-saving, too. Whatever lighting you choose, sleek, understated designs are best not only for aesthetic but also for practical reasons: in the first place, less dust can gather, and they are easier to clean than lights with intricate detailing.

accessories

right
A chalkboard is great for keeping track of what you need to stock up on the next time you go shopping.

below
Tea towels no longer come only in white with a blue stripe: there are myriad beautiful designs to brighten up your kitchen.

opposite, top
A selection of hooks is essential for aprons, tea towels and bags filled with such necessaries as fresh cleaning cloths or pegs.

O n the whole, the kitchen isn't the place for artwork: space on the walls is too precious (it could be hung with extra storage), and pictures are just something else that needs cleaning periodically. So consider how you can inject character into the room without investing in non-essentials.

Small appliances – especially those that are used daily, such as the kettle, coffee-maker or toaster – often find their permanent homes on the worktop. With that in mind, choose models that are easy on the eye, perhaps with a bit of a retro vibe, or in an appealing shade. Take a similar approach with tea towels and oven gloves, and hang attractive, colourful designs from a simple Shaker-style peg rack.

Other useful accessories that might not be immediately obvious are chalkboards (perfect for noting down a shopping list as comestibles run out), hooks (handy for everything from aprons to shopping bags) and some kind of noticeboard (for such important items as theatre tickets and loyalty-card vouchers).

at-a-glance guide

DO THINK ABOUT THE LAYOUT OF YOUR HOME AND THE WAY YOUR KITCHEN RELATES TO OTHER SPACES.

DO CHOOSE A COLOUR THAT SUITS THE ASPECT OF THE ROOM, AS WELL AS YOUR PERSONAL TASTE.

DO SELECT SURFACES THAT ARE DURABLE AND EASY TO CLEAN.

DO BUY THE BEST KITCHEN FURNITURE YOU CAN AFFORD.

DO INVEST IN CHOPPING BOARDS AND TRIVETS TO PROTECT YOUR SURFACES.

DO CONSIDER ADDING A KITCHEN TABLE AND CHAIRS, IF YOU HAVE THE SPACE.

DO PUT MORE SHELVES INTO YOUR EXISTING FITTED UNITS.

DO INVEST IN WALL-HUNG STORAGE.

DO SPECIFY AN EXCELLENT EXTRACTION SYSTEM, ESPECIALLY IF YOUR KITCHEN IS OPEN-PLAN.

DO MAKE THE MOST OF ANY NATURAL LIGHT.

DO PLAN A LIGHTING SCHEME THAT PROVIDES BOTH AMBIENT AND TASK LIGHTING.

DO SEARCH OUT SMALL APPLIANCES THAT ARE AS AESTHETICALLY PLEASING AS THEY ARE PRACTICAL.

DO HAVE A CHALKBOARD FOR LISTS, AND A NOTICEBOARD FOR KEEPING NOTES AND TICKETS HANDY.

DON'T FORGET TO MAKE SURE THAT YOUR KITCHEN LAYOUT ADHERES TO THE PRINCIPLE OF THE 'WORKING TRIANGLE'.

DON'T GET TOO HUNG UP ON THE LATEST TRENDS; OPT INSTEAD FOR LASTING STYLE.

DON'T USE A PAINT THAT ISN'T SPECIFICALLY FORMULATED FOR THE KITCHEN ENVIRONMENT.

DON'T SPEND MONEY ON PULL-OUT LARDERS OR MAGIC CORNERS UNLESS YOU DON'T MIND THEM BEING DIFFICULT TO CLEAN.

DON'T PUT REGULARLY USED UTENSILS IN A DRAWER: POP THEM INTO A POT ON THE WORKTOP.

DON'T FORGET THAT CEILING RACKS ARE SPACE-SAVING AND CONVENIENT.

DON'T CHOOSE FUSSY FABRIC WINDOW DRESSINGS, AS THEY'LL JUST COLLECT DUST AND GREASE.

DON'T RELY ON AMBIENT LIGHTING. WORKING IN YOUR OWN SHADOW WHEN PREPARING FOOD CAN LEAD TO ACCIDENTS.

DON'T GO TOO LONG WITHOUT GIVING YOUR KITCHEN A CLUTTER CLEAR-OUT.

bathroom

Over the last decade or so a lot has been said in the media about bathrooms becoming more akin to spas – a space for relaxation, as well as daily ablutions. However, with our busy modern lives, is it realistic to manage a long soak in the tub any more than once a month? With that in mind, we should first focus on creating a functional space that makes our morning and evening routines easier: in the end, that will probably have a greater positive impact on our stress levels.

left
Thanks to the use of compact, contemporary sanitaryware, this tiny bathroom is both stylish and practical.

below
Building a half-height partition wall between the WC and the bath has enabled these two facilities to be placed closer together than would otherwise have been possible.

U nless you're planning to remodel your space completely, you probably won't have a lot of control over the layout; in fact, even if you are having a new bathroom fitted, you may not be able to rearrange the fittings if the room is small. It's difficult to go far wrong with what goes where, not least because you'll usually be relying on someone with experience to fit the sanitaryware, but do be careful not to squeeze things in too tightly. You need a bit of room around everything in order to use the facilities comfortably, so if you need to, opt for one of the space-saving bathroom ranges that are available.

happy home hint

CHOOSE AS LARGE A MIRROR AS POSSIBLE, NOT JUST SO THAT YOU CAN SEE YOUR OWN BEAMING FACE, BUT ALSO TO REFLECT LIGHT BACK INTO THE ROOM. IF POSSIBLE, POSITION IT NEAR THE WINDOW, TO GET THE BENEFIT OF NATURAL LIGHT DURING THE DAY. MAKE SURE YOU HAVE MIRROR LIGHTING FOR AFTER DARK, TOO.

colour

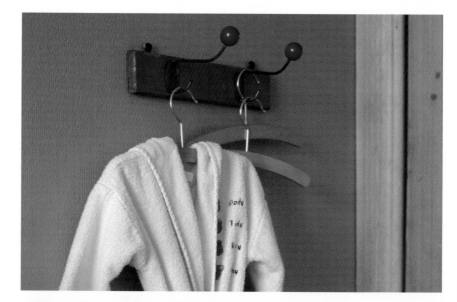

Before picking up a paintbrush, think carefully about the mood you want to create. To evoke that get-up-and-go feeling during your morning shower, bring in a fresh, zingy shade, such as lime green – but remember to use bold colours with a light touch. Alternatively, if your daily routine dictates that you bathe in the evening in order to wind down before bed, stick to muted tones and neutrals. White is classic – and the best option for sanitaryware, to ensure it doesn't look dated a decade down the line – but an all-white bathroom can look a bit clinical, so either pick an accent shade or, at the very least, try to incorporate some differing textures.

right
A bold use of cheerful colour prevents this almost entirely white bathroom from seeming cold and clinical.

right, top
The cherry red of these hooks provides a pop of colour against the green–blue background.

opposite
Natural timber gives this bathroom an Alpine feel of rustic elegance.

walls and floors

opposite
Partially restricted ceiling
height is less troublesome
in a bathroom than
elsewhere, provided the
layout is well designed.

right
Tiles laid in a brick pattern
lend a charmingly retro
feel, particularly if coloured
grout is used for emphasis.

below
Large tiles create a
contemporary look, and
the use of the same design
on walls and floor gives
the illusion of space.

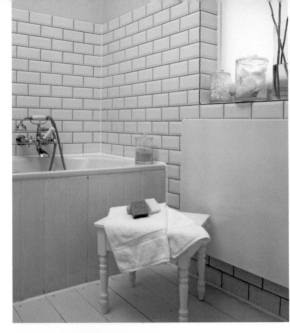

The air in the bathroom will inevitably become very humid, no matter how effective your extractor unit, so it's imperative that you use a paint specifically designed for bathrooms, and it's probably best to steer clear of wallpaper. In wet zones, such as in showers and behind basins, tiles are the most common solution for walls and floors. Large-format designs are a great choice, as fewer grout lines mean quicker cleaning, and remember that tinted grout will make life easier still, as it doesn't discolour so obviously. Also available are waterproof panel systems, which are even more straightforward to maintain at their best; back-painted glass gives a fantastic luminescent effect, or – if budget is no object – a sheet of marble or granite will ensure a luxurious look.

Carpet is not suitable for the floor; opt instead for something waterproof and non-slip. Ceramic tiles are hard-wearing and inexpensive, but, unless you're planning to install underfloor heating, they can be a little chilly on a winter's morning (as can stone, which is attractive and durable, but also expensive, and will require sealing). Vinyl and rubber are warmer on the toes, and are available in a wide range of designs and colours, while timber is also comfortable underfoot, although it must be sealed properly to avoid water damage.

furniture

left
A step in front of the sink is a handy addition if you have small children.

below
Vintage pieces can be adapted for use as vanity units.

opposite
Matching freestanding and fitted furniture maximizes both style and storage space.

If you are remodelling, try to pick sanitaryware that works with fitted furniture. A back-to-wall WC with a cistern concealed in a cabinet not only looks slick but also makes cleaning more straightforward (no more reaching behind the loo), while a vanity unit hides all the basin pipework as well as providing storage space. Designs on legs, or ones that are wall-hung, will give the illusion of more space, but floor-standing cabinets with plinths make cleaning easier, as dust can't hide under the units.

Many people simply don't have room in their bathroom for additional furnishings. But even if you're lucky enough to have plenty of space, there isn't much you can add that will enhance your experience of the bathroom: maybe a chair (handy when dressing), or a cupboard to provide storage as an alternative to the more usual wall-hung bathroom cabinet. Do consider the damp, steamy nature of the room when choosing pieces for it; this is not the place for cherished fine antiques.

bathroom

storage

right
The provision of plenty
of hooks for towels will
ensure that you don't
spend your life picking
them up from the floor.

below
Open shelves are an
affordable option – but
consider hiding the clutter
behind curtains.

below, right
If you keep toiletries
tucked away, cleaning the
bathroom will be much
quicker and easier.

Every room in the house benefits from having clutter hidden from view, but nowhere is this truer than in the bathroom. A large collection of lotions and potions on the side of the bath (or on the windowsill) not only looks less than desirable, but also considerably slows down cleaning. It is crucial to have ample storage, and a sizeable wall cabinet is essential; maybe even two, one for toiletries and one for loo roll and cleaning products. It's helpful, too, to have a shelf to keep shampoo and shower gel within easy reach when bathing, but keep the number of bottles and tubes here to a minimum, since you'll have to move them every time you clean.

soft furnishings

below, left
If you plan to have a rug in your bathroom, first make sure that its colours are waterproof by testing an inconspicuous area.

below
Bath towels come in more than just plain colours these days, so have some fun choosing the designs.

Apart from towels and a bath mat (which don't quite count), soft furnishings don't really have a place in the bathroom because of the moist air, which can cause mould and mildew. For this reason, choose window treatments that can stand up to the steamy atmosphere, or, if your window isn't overlooked, simply rely on obscure glazing. If you can't resist a cushion or two, or have your heart set on curtains, make sure you have a powerful extractor fan, and only ever use washable fabrics.

bathroom
lighting

A bove all, make sure the lights you use in your bathroom are specifically designed for use there. The high humidity means that it's not safe to use just any fitting (this is also the reason pull-switches are necessary, rather than conventional wall-mounted switches).

Whatever combination of spot, pendant and wall lights you choose, the light should be as even and natural as possible; after all, if you don't have good light in which to do your hair or make-up, you don't get an accurate view of how you look to others when you're out and about. For the best effect, choose mirror lighting with daylight bulbs. If you plan to use your bathroom for relaxation as well as more perfunctory bathing, it's a good idea to have a lighting scheme with mood options: a bright one for waking you up in the morning, and a muted alternative for long soaks in the bathtub.

opposite, top
Good natural light is
a must near a mirror,
especially if you normally
do your make-up in the
bathroom.

below
Lights around the mirror are
essential for evening and
early-morning preparation.

right
Make the most of both
natural and artificial light
by including a large mirror
or a mirrored cabinet.

bathroom accessories

right
Bathtime toys keep little ones amused, and a padded seat means comfort is assured for Mum or Dad.

below
Make sure that any ornaments you choose to put in the bathroom can cope with the humidity.

Practical additions to the basic bathroom include hooks for bathrobes and clothes (don't skimp: more really is more in this instance), a laundry basket for catching cast-offs at source, a foot-friendly bathmat and, of course, a set of the thickest, fluffiest Egyptian cotton towels you can find.

Many people prefer to keep their bathrooms fairly free of decorative bits and bobs, because of the moisture and for ease of cleaning, but one or two carefully chosen pieces can prevent the space from seeming too clinical. Of course, if you chose the essential elements of the bathroom for their aesthetic value – some particularly glorious tiles, say, or a beautiful vintage cabinet or statuesque reclaimed bathtub – it's best to let them remain the centre of attention without drawing the eye away.

at-a-glance guide

happy home hint

Heated towel rails really make a difference, and warm, dry, fluffy towels are the measure of a bathroom that's a pleasure to use. Make sure you choose one with enough space for everyone's towels, and always opt for the variety with an electrical connection, so that you can use it in the summer, when the central heating is off.

DO opt for a back-to-wall WC, since there'll be no reaching behind it to clean.

DO choose a basin with a vanity unit, for storage and simpler cleaning in one fell swoop.

DO use strong colours with a light touch.

DO stick to white sanitaryware.

DO consider large-format tiles and tinted grout for easier cleaning.

DO make sure your choice of floor-covering is non-slip, with a warm foot-feel.

DO have a shelf within easy reach of the bath or shower for such daily essentials as shampoo.

DO specify a powerful extraction unit.

DO hang your mirror as close to the window as possible, and have mirror lighting, too.

DON'T pick oversized sanitaryware for a small space. Compact ranges are available.

DON'T select a delicate wallpaper; in fact, if it's a very steamy room, don't choose wallpaper at all.

DON'T use paint finishes that aren't intended for use in the bathroom.

DON'T rule out sheet materials, such as back-painted glass or stone fascias.

DON'T use carpet in the bathroom.

DON'T include decorative items that can be damaged by water or steam.

DON'T underestimate how much storage you'll need.

DON'T fit lights that aren't rated for use in the bathroom.

DON'T rely on a single central ceiling light, and avoid unflattering fluorescent bulbs.

bedroom

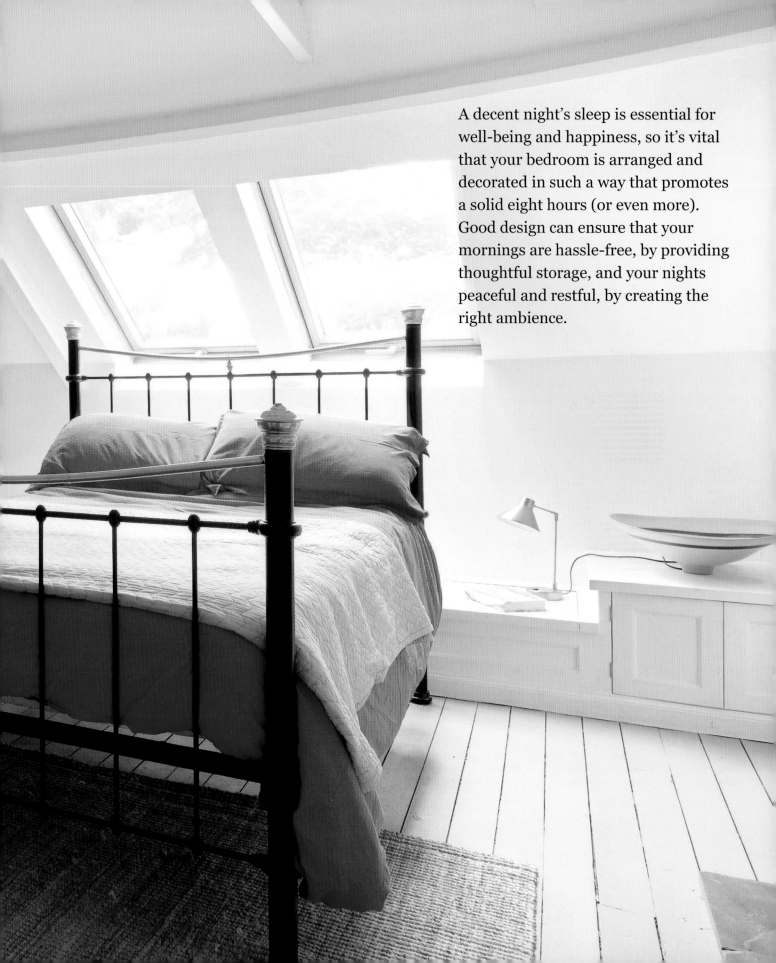

A decent night's sleep is essential for well-being and happiness, so it's vital that your bedroom is arranged and decorated in such a way that promotes a solid eight hours (or even more). Good design can ensure that your mornings are hassle-free, by providing thoughtful storage, and your nights peaceful and restful, by creating the right ambience.

W hether your space is large or small, there are a few rules to bear in mind when it comes to what goes where. For example, your bed should be positioned such that you (and your partner) can get into and out of it with ease – so it should never have its long side against a wall. This not only means that there's no need to clamber over a sleeping person when making a night-time trip to get a glass of water, but also allows a bedside table or cabinet on both sides.

It's worth thinking about which wall to put the headboard against. If you have noisy neighbours, the party wall isn't the best choice (but it would be a good idea to install soundproofing anyway). Another situation to avoid is near a draughty window, although you really ought to remedy the draught in any case, to improve comfort and lower your heating bill.

When it comes to other furnishings there's no optimum layout, although if you share the bedroom with a partner, it's usually best to place each person's clothes storage on the relevant side of the bed. Whatever furniture you choose for this space, make sure there is ample room to access chests and cupboards without drawers or doors knocking against another piece.

opposite
If you're able to position your bed so that you wake up to a fabulous view every morning, then so much the better.

left, top
If your bedroom is narrow, aim to find a bed that allows you to do away with bedside tables.

left
Try to keep your bed away from the doorway (or doorways, if you have an en suite), to keep access easy.

bedroom

colour

below
Pink and red might not be the obvious combination, but, sometimes, throwing away the rule book can produce amazing results.

below, right
If you're mixing patterns, try to stick to a palette of colours in similar tones, to ensure balance.

opposite
A pale background scheme is calming, and provides a fantastic backdrop for bright accessories.

Some people like strong colour in the bedroom, as they feel it reflects passion and vitality, but in fact restful shades are often best. Choose colours that make you feel calm and secure: pale to middling blues and greens are popular, but make sure you choose a soft shade that isn't too chilly. Duck-egg blue and sage green fit the bill nicely, while some of the warmer whites (with the slightest hint of yellow, red or brown in them) also do a great job of creating a cosy feel without resorting to strong colour.

Of course, you can keep the wall colour entirely neutral and introduce interest with materials: natural wood has a warm appearance, while the textures of wool-rich carpet, a floaty voile or a velvety bed throw can give a tactile dimension to a room dressed entirely in white.

silence

kiss her
it
might
be
your
last
chance

KISS

walls and floors

right
The style of these floor-to-ceiling cupboards is echoed in the design of the doors – an elegant touch.

right, bottom
Here, walls and floors painted in pale colours allow the rich tones of the timber furniture to take centre stage.

There's no getting around it: carpet is excellent in bedrooms, because it eliminates draughts and is soft on bare feet. The height of soft floor-covering luxury is one with a high wool content, but other natural fibres have become popular in recent years. Of all the plant-based options, jute is the softest, and therefore the most appropriate.

However, those in hotter climes might prefer the cool feel of tile or timber, but take note: if you have stripped floorboards in your bedroom, watch out for splinters and nails standing proud of the surface. If you have a hard floor, it's worth placing a soft rug by your bed, so that your toes are cosseted when you get up in the morning.

opposite
A large, foot-friendly rug will help to make a hard floor welcoming to your toes first thing in the morning.

bedroom
furniture

right
This hall stand is a quirky piece to use in a bedroom – but ideal for hanging up the next day's outfit.

below
Fitted storage makes the best use of awkwardly shaped rooms, particularly those with sloping ceilings.

Arguably the most important piece of furniture is your bed, since you spend about a third of your life in it. Buy the biggest you can, especially if you have to share it with someone who's prone to changing sleeping position a lot in the night, but don't buy one so big that you have trouble fitting in other furnishings. Low designs have a more contemporary feel, and are great for small rooms, as they don't dominate so much. However, they don't boast the same sort of under-bed storage capacity as many taller examples.

Whatever bed you choose, you'll need to replace your mattress every ten years to ensure optimum support and comfort, which are essential for a good night's sleep. The most traditional and common type of mattress is the sprung variety, of which those with pocket springs are considered the best. Other options include memory foam for super-softness, or even a waterbed, which is like sleeping in an almost weightless state (but it is more expensive, and you do have to adjust to what is at first a slightly weird sensation).

If you have no fitted storage, you'll need to think about wardrobes and chests of drawers for

storing hanging and folded garments. You might also consider a dressing table for doing hair and make-up (near a power socket, to ensure easy use of a hairdryer). A simple wooden chair for throwing clothes over could be useful, or add a more comfortable upholstered option for quiet moments when you're not chilling out in bed; it could be the perfect sanctuary in a busy family home. If you're lacking a linen cupboard, consider a chest placed in the traditional position at the foot of the bed, as it's a handy and logical place to store bedlinen and blankets.

left, top
Vintage shop fittings are great for bedroom storage. Just make sure you keep the contents tidy if the piece is glass-fronted.

left
It's an excellent idea to invest in a bed design that incorporates some sort of storage.

happy home hint

TELEVISIONS SEEM TO BE IN EVERY ROOM NOW; YOU CAN EVEN BUY WATERPROOF ONES FOR THE BATHROOM. BUT IT'S A GOOD IDEA TO BANISH THEM FROM THE BEDROOM, BECAUSE IF YOU START TO ASSOCIATE GOING TO BED WITH ENTERTAINMENT, YOU'LL FIND IT DIFFICULT TO FALL ASLEEP.

storage

left
Hide clutter on open shelves with matching or contrasting boxes and files.

below
The mezzanine level in this unusual space is cunningly used as an area for clothes storage and dressing.

opposite
If you have the space, using a whole room as a wardrobe is a wonderful luxury.

hether you have a capsule wardrobe or a shoe collection to rival that of Imelda Marcos, storage for clothes and accessories is going to be your biggest concern in the bedroom. Fitted wardrobes offer the best use of space; in small rooms, fit sliding doors, since you don't need to allow room for the door to swing open.

But just because you can close the door and all looks neat and tidy, it doesn't mean you shouldn't arrange your belongings carefully inside. Any storage will work much harder for you if it's organized, and you'll find it quicker to get out of the house in the morning, too, since everything will be just where you expect it to be. Keep like garments with like garments, folded neatly or hung on their own hanger (not the wire variety, though, or your clothes could get misshapen).

Whatever type of wardrobe you buy, if you have a particularly large collection of clothes, shoes and accessories, you may find yourself unable to fit everything in. In this case, try separating your winter and summer garments, and place out-of-season items elsewhere, possibly in underbed storage boxes or vacuum bags. Remember, too, that not all shoes need to be kept in the bedroom. Daily

bedroom

right
A dressing table should
have space to store your
cosmetics and jewellery, so
that they're close at hand
when you need them.

far right
This loft-conversion
bedroom cleverly uses
the space under the eaves
for built-in storage.

favourites are best stored near the front door, so they're easily to hand as you leave the house.

Underbed storage is the secret weapon of the well-organized bedroom: you can stow a surprising amount of stuff under what is often the biggest piece of furniture in the room. For ease of cleaning, the best type is within a divan, or a specially designed bed with integrated drawers, so that the dust is kept out and you won't have to suffer the major task of dragging everything out to vacuum under the bed. That said, however, large boxes with wheels can make the job easier, if you just can't be without the traditional charms of a bedstead. Try to store only items that aren't used often, to avoid having to get down to floor level every day.

It's also a good idea to fix hooks in handy places, not just for dressing gowns, but also so that you can hang up your outfit for the next day, or store such accessories as bags, hats and scarves. Smaller rows of hooks are great for such costume jewellery as necklaces and bracelets, and the bonus is that these trinkets become decorative items in the context of the room, not just when they're being worn.

happy home hint

MOST OF US AREN'T ENTIRELY HAPPY WITH WHAT WE SEE IN THE MIRROR, BUT THAT'S NO REASON NOT TO HAVE A FULL-LENGTH ONE IN YOUR BEDROOM. BEING ABLE TO SEE YOUR WHOLE REFLECTION MEANS YOU CAN MORE EASILY JUDGE WHETHER AN OUTFIT SUITS YOU OR NOT, AND WILL GIVE YOU GREATER CONFIDENCE.

bedroom

soft furnishings

Crucial to a good night's sleep is a window treatment that blocks out light, especially if you live in a part of the world that enjoys particularly long hours of daylight in the summer. But remember that you also need to be able to draw it right back (or up) so that you can benefit from plenty of natural light when you're not asleep. Seeing clearly is key to a perfect coiffure or an elegantly coordinated outfit, after all. Lined curtains are best, or why not use a special blackout blind?

Duvets have become more popular than traditional sheets and blankets in recent times, as they're cosy and snuggly, and it's easier to make the bed. However, blankets can be decorative and flexible (you can layer them, so there's no need to change tog rating with the seasons), and there's also something comforting about their old-fashionedness.

left
Try layering your bed with blankets and throws, rather than choosing the more usual duvet option.

below
Pets and white bedlinen don't mix, so a coloured throw over your bed can be a good idea.

Patchwork is perfect for cottage chic, and it's not difficult to make yourself.

If you're going for the modern option, natural-fibre duvets are best (feather or silk), not just because they're warmer than those with synthetic fillings, but also because they're breathable, so you're less likely to wake up feeling clammy. The same goes for pillows, although memory foam is a wonderfully supportive option, and one that's good for those who have allergies and can't bear feather fillings. Consider buying a duvet bigger than the size of your bed (a king size if you have a double bed, for example), and if you sleep with a partner, you might want to have two separate single duvets.

The natural-materials rule also applies to bedlinen. Silk is wantonly sumptuous, but has a price tag to match, and linen is luxurious but also fairly pricy (although good-quality linen lasts a lifetime and actually improves with age), so cotton is the fibre of choice for many. Check that the thread count is 180 or greater (200 or above is even better), to ensure you're buying decent quality.

Handcrafted pieces, such as this crocheted blanket, embroidered cushion and handmade toy owl, add a homely, comforting touch.

lighting

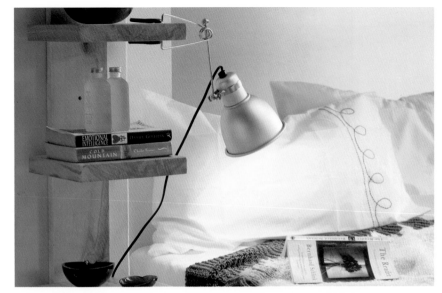

I f you have a standard pendant light fitting, make sure it doesn't hang too low if it's positioned over the bed, as you don't want there to be any danger of hitting it with the duvet when making the bed – or indeed with your arm, if engaging in a particularly emphatic stretch. A dimmer switch is a good idea, so that you can turn the light levels soothingly down as you get ready for bed, and also aren't shocked into wakefulness immediately the light is flicked on in the morning.

Task lighting is covered by the bedside lamp or lamps, and possibly by another on the dressing table if you need it for your toilette; a daylight bulb would be a benefit in the latter. Wall-fixed reading lights are very useful, as they provide directional illumination without the glare from the bulb catching the corner of your eye, although the bedside variety is fine as long as it's both directional and adjustable.

right, top
An adjustable lamp by your bed is invaluable if you like to read for a while before dropping off to sleep.

right
Always get vintage lamps checked by an electrician before you plug them in.

accessories

To maintain a restful feel, many people prefer to keep practical accessories to a minimum, but a bedside alarm clock is often a necessity for those with busy lives (although it can't really be described as adding to the restful feel). Choose one that also functions as a radio and a dock for a music player, so that you don't need separate units; this minimizes not only financial outlay but also dusting.

Other useful accoutrements to have by the bed include a coaster or two for that morning cup of tea or night-time glass of water, and a bookmark for your bedtime reading. Also keep a spare blanket near by (in case you feel chilly in the night), and have your slippers and dressing gown to hand for when you get up.

right
In a small room, less is more. Keep the accessories to a minimum in order to preserve a sense of space.

right, top
If there isn't room for a wardrobe in a guest room, just providing somewhere to hang clothes will be enough.

opposite, top
Pictures don't have to be big to make an impact: a collection of smaller pieces grouped together can be equally stylish.

at-a-glance guide

DO POSITION YOUR CLOTHES STORAGE ON YOUR SIDE OF THE BED.

DO CHOOSE A CALMING AND COMFORTING PAINT SHADE OR WALLPAPER DESIGN.

DO USE TEXTURE TO INTRODUCE INTEREST IF YOU'RE PLANNING A RESTRICTED COLOUR SCHEME.

DO BUY THE BIGGEST AND BEST BED THAT FITS BOTH THE ROOM AND YOUR BUDGET.

DO CHOOSE A SOFT, FOOT-FRIENDLY FLOOR-COVERING, SUCH AS CARPET, OR MAKE USE OF TACTILE RUGS.

DO INCLUDE STORAGE FOR BEDLINEN.

DO PLAN SOME KIND OF UNDERBED STORAGE.

DO OPT FOR BESPOKE FITTED STORAGE IF YOUR SPACE AND FUNDS WILL ALLOW.

DO USE HOOKS FOR DRESSING GOWNS, BAGS, SCARVES, JEWELLERY AND OTHER ACCESSORIES.

DO CHOOSE WINDOW DRESSINGS THAT WILL KEEP DAYLIGHT OUT.

DO FIT A DIMMER SWITCH.

DON'T PUT YOUR BED BY A DRAUGHTY WINDOW, ALONG A WALL OR AGAINST A PARTY WALL.

DON'T CHOOSE BRIGHT, STIMULATING SHADES FOR THE WALLS.

DON'T FORGET TO CHECK FOR SPLINTERS AND PROTRUDING NAILS IN STRIPPED FLOORBOARDS.

DON'T GO FOR LONGER THAN TEN YEARS WITHOUT REPLACING YOUR MATTRESS.

DON'T RELY ON YOUR WARDROBE DOOR TO HIDE THE CLUTTER: STORAGE IS MORE EFFECTIVE IF IT'S PROPERLY ORGANIZED.

DON'T STORE OFTEN-USED ITEMS UNDER THE BED.

DON'T KEEP ALL YOUR SHOES IN THE BEDROOM. SOME ARE BETTER HOUSED NEAR THE FRONT OR BACK DOOR.

DON'T UNDERESTIMATE THE VALUE OF SPLITTING YOUR WARDROBE INTO 'SUMMER' AND 'WINTER' AND STORING IT AS SUCH.

DON'T BUY CHEAP BEDLINEN, OR ANYTHING MADE FROM SYNTHETIC FIBRES.

DON'T CHOOSE NON-DIRECTIONAL BEDSIDE LAMPS IF YOU LIKE TO READ AT NIGHT.

DON'T CROWD SURFACES WITH DECORATIVE ORNAMENTS. THE IDEA IS TO KEEP THIS ROOM CALM AND TRANQUIL.

child's room

Every child needs a space to call theirs, whether it's part of a room shared with siblings or a room of their very own. As soon as they're old enough to express an opinion, they should be involved in choosing their own furnishings and decor. As they grow up, their needs will change, and their surroundings should be adjusted accordingly.

layout

happy
home hint

PROVIDE DECORATION FOR YOUR
CHILD'S ROOM, AND ENCOURAGE
THEIR SENSE OF SELF-WORTH
AND ANY ARTISTIC LEANINGS, BY
FRAMING THEIR ARTWORK AND
HANGING IT UP. CHOOSE SIMPLE
FRAMES (A SLIM BLACK PROFILE
WORKS BRILLIANTLY) IN STANDARD
SIZES (A4 BEING THE MOST
COMMON), SO IT'S EASY TO SWITCH
IN NEW WORK NEXT TIME
YOUR CHILD CREATES SOMETHING
THEY'RE PROUD OF.

S afety is paramount, so make sure that furnishings don't impinge on the most frequently used routes around the room. Children often dash about, so narrow spaces can become a hazard. Also, position the bed away from the window, so that they can't climb on to the windowsill, and from wall-hung shelves, so that bed-bouncing (or just standing on the mattress) doesn't result in a head injury.

Unlike a double, which needs to be placed so that either occupant can get up in the middle of the night without disturbing the other, a single bed can go lengthways against the wall. This not only gives less opportunity for falling out of bed, but also ensures that as much floor space as possible is available for playing.

Remember that your child's play area doesn't necessarily have to be in their bedroom. If space is at a premium, you could designate a patch of floor in the living room or kitchen (where you can keep an eye on them), or, if you're particularly blessed with square footage, you might even be able to have a separate playroom.

Particular layout problems can occur if siblings share a room, since it's important to create separate zones for each child. This divide could be visual rather than physical: you could simply use different colours and patterns to mark out whose territory is whose.

below
A freestanding set of shelves can make a brilliant room divider, demarcating areas for rest and play.

opposite
Bunk beds – either built-in or freestanding – are great for smaller spaces.

colour

left
Keep the background scheme neutral, and add colour with accessories, so that your child's room can easily grow up with them.

opposite, left
A lick of paint can transform a dated piece of furniture into something fun and funky.

opposite, right
Let older children choose the colour scheme and style they like, so that they can express their own personality.

When you ask them to think of schemes for kids' rooms, many parents think of brights, because they associate jolly colours with a fun and playful atmosphere. It's not actually the best route to take, however. Sensory overstimulation, and a feeling of excitement, isn't a great environment in which to teach your children good sleeping habits.

White (or off-white) is a versatile backdrop that will stand the test of time. Updated every now and then with new pictures, fresh curtains and bedlinen, and possibly different furnishings, this type of simple scheme can last a child right through to their teenage years and beyond. It can be accessorized with plains or patterns, pastels or splashes of more vivid shades. However, if neutrals aren't for you, try a gorgeous turquoise (a great foil for primary colours), lavender or duck-egg blue.

walls and floors

left
Stripped floorboards
are hard-wearing, but
a soft rug makes it more
comfortable for little ones
to sit on the floor.

opposite
Floor paint is a durable
finish for hard floors, and
is available in a wide variety
of shades.

Whether horizontal or vertical, the rule of thumb for surfaces is 'easy to clean'. Then it won't matter if your little angel empties a pot of poster paint on the floor, or manages to get sticky fingerprints up the wall: a quick wipe will be all that's needed.

For the walls, paint is preferable to wallpaper, as it's simpler to update, less fussy and (provided you choose an enduring formula) much easier to keep looking its best. Murals can be charming, but do bear in mind that when the child gets older, they may think the design 'babyish' and want to have it painted over.

Smooth floor surfaces are better for play, as well as being more washable. Toy cars don't roll very well on carpet, while small soldiers or dolls simply fall over, so consider rubber tiles, laminate or wood. You could even brighten up a concrete sub-floor using a special type of paint. However, hard floors can be chilly and uncomfortable to sit or crawl on, so add a big, soft rug, especially if your child is still young and spends a lot of time playing on the floor.

opposite
Painted furniture can be
wiped clean easily, and
updated with fresh paint
in a different colour when
your child's tastes change.

left
Plastic furniture is bright,
cheerful and, most
importantly, washable.

below
Vintage or antique pieces
are lovely in a child's room,
but make sure they can
stand up to the rigours
of their situation.

There are lots of furniture ranges aimed at new (and not-so-new) parents, but they don't always offer good value. Classic pieces that can be painted or dressed differently as the child grows up are often a much better long-term investment. For example, don't buy a specialist nappy-changing unit, as you won't need it for long. Choose a chest of drawers of the right height, and simply top it with a wipe-clean, padded changing mat.

This approach to furnishing children's rooms also avoids the 'latest fad' trap. Beware of buying items branded with cartoon characters or television programmes, since you could find yourself replacing something expensive to avoid the tantrums that inevitably occur when the characters fall out of favour. Also, try not to be persuaded into 'fun' furniture – a bed shaped like a racing car or a rocket, for example – since, for good sleep habits, bedtime shouldn't be associated with excitement.

The most important thing when choosing furniture is to ensure that it's robust, because it will inevitably get jumped on and bashed, probably fairly frequently. Freestanding furniture is safest fixed to the wall, especially lighter pieces, so that there's no danger of them falling over if they are climbed on. It's also because of the wear and tear kids' furniture receives (not just the fact that they look cheerful) that painted pieces are a good idea, since they can be retouched or even fully repainted periodically to spruce them up, as well as to alter their appeal as the child gets older.

storage

Most important here is ease of access. If the child can easily locate the toy they're looking for, they won't cause chaos trying to find it; and making it simple for them to pack their belongings away will help them learn how to tidy up after playtime. So plan low-level storage options, such as a toy chest, baskets and boxes placed on the floor, easily reached rows of hooks and bookshelves at child height.

Tiny children don't need a wardrobe, since most of their clothes can be stored folded, but do make sure older children have space to hang their clothes. Encourage order (and speedy dressing) by storing garments of the same type together, maybe even designating separate shelves, drawers or boxes for T-shirts, skirts, jumpers and jeans; labels will serve as a reminder to keep things tidy, too. In addition, separating things in this way (not just clothes, but also toys and other belongings) will ensure that you don't end up with one big jumble of 'stuff', which often results in items being mislaid or getting broken.

opposite, top
Bits and bobs can avoid
becoming clutter if you
use storage boxes.

opposite, bottom
Hooks are a good idea,
since they make putting
clothes and accessories
away that much easier.

right
Store toys on low
shelves, for accessibility,
and delicate items and
ornaments higher up,
where damage is less likely.

happy home hint

IF THEY'RE BUSY LOOKING FOR
A SPECIFIC ITEM IN A CUPBOARD
FULL OF TOYS, CHILDREN WILL
TIP EVERYTHING ON TO THE
FLOOR UNTIL THEY FIND IT. SO
MAKE LIFE EASIER FOR THEM:
KEEP SIMILAR TOYS IN CLEAR
STORAGE BOXES, SO THE CHILD
CAN SEE WHAT'S INSIDE
WITHOUT CAUSING CHAOS.

soft furnishings

opposite
Florals, stripes and spots combine easily for a pretty, vintage-style appeal.

left
Seek out simple, colourful, modern printed cottons, and have duvet and cushion covers made up.

below
A patterned rug in bold colours, like this cheerful striped example, will keep its good looks longer than paler, plainer designs.

Whatever furnishings you use, make sure they're easy to clean. Cushion covers, curtains and bedspreads should all be able to be thrown into the washing machine, while washable loose covers are ideal for upholstered furniture and beanbags. Good-quality cotton is best, since it washes well and is robust enough to stand up to the inevitable rough-and-tumble. Patterns are also preferable to plains: they don't look grubby so quickly, and, should you find you can't get a stain out, it won't be too obvious.

Window dressings are particularly important in a child's bedroom, since being able to block out daylight makes nap time and summer nights much more peaceful. A blackout blind can work wonders if you're struggling to get your child to sleep because it's still light outside at bedtime, but curtains, either made with thick fabric or lined with a special blackout lining, do the job just as effectively. Safety should be uppermost in your mind: ensure blind cords are wound over a hook attached to the wall (a child could strangle themselves if they started playing with them and then lost their balance), and don't opt for floor-skimming curtains (a trip hazard, if ever there was one).

Soft furnishings are also a good place in which to indulge your child's hankering for the latest craze, since they're relatively easy and inexpensive to replace once the fad has passed.

lighting

Dimmer switches are a benefit all over the house, but the child's bedroom is where they really come into their own. Not only will one let you check on your baby in the middle of the night without waking them up, but also, if you have older children, you can turn the lights down bit by bit to make a gentle distinction between playtime and bedtime.

Lots of fun lighting options are available aimed at children: you could go for a funky lava lamp for a boy's pad, twinkly fairy lights for a princess's palace, or a rotating lamp that projects stars on to the walls for a nursery. However, do bear in mind that you don't want to create too much excitement at night-time. A soothing twinkle is fine; flashing disco lights really aren't. Young children, or those who are still rather afraid of the dark, will benefit from having a night light of some kind, while older kids and teenagers will appreciate a reading lamp.

opposite, top left
Little girls love the twinkly,
decorative effect that can be
achieved with strategically
placed fairy lights.

opposite, top right
The long desk in this shared
room features a workstation
for each child, with a lamp
as an essential element.

opposite, bottom
Fabric lampshades can
be changed easily and
inexpensively to suit
your child's tastes as
they grow up.

right
An adjustable lamp by the
bed is important, whether
for bedtime stories or
independent reading.

accessories

A ccessories probably aren't something you'll be short of. Toys and other gifts from family and friends begin to amass the minute your bundle of joy comes into the world, and, when they're old enough, your child will soon tell you what they want in their space.

But there are some pieces that will augment a child's room. Hooks for hanging pyjamas, dressing gowns, bags and other accessories – maybe even the next day's outfit – can be very handy indeed, while a pinboard makes a great place to display drawings, photographs and postcards. Children love to display their collections of things, so find a way to let them do this.

above
If your child takes part in competitions, provide a place for them to display their rosettes, trophies or medals.

right
Who needs ornaments when you have a cheerful collection of colourful toys on show?

at-a-glance guide

DO CONSIDER SAFETY AT EVERY TURN.

DO PUT SINGLE BEDS LENGTHWAYS ALONG A WALL TO LEAVE AS MUCH SPACE AS POSSIBLE FOR PLAY.

DO THINK ABOUT HOW YOU CAN CREATE SEPARATE PERSONAL ZONES IN SHARED ROOMS, EITHER PHYSICALLY OR VISUALLY.

DO GET YOUR CHILD INVOLVED IN CHOOSING DECOR AND FURNISHINGS FOR THEIR ROOM.

DO ADD COMFORT TO HARD FLOORS WITH RUGS, BLANKETS, CUSHIONS AND BEANBAGS.

DO CHOOSE ROBUST FURNISHINGS.

DO OPT FOR PAINTED FURNITURE, SINCE IT CAN BE REDECORATED TO SUIT A CHILD'S CHANGING TASTE.

DO MAKE STORAGE AS EASY TO ACCESS AS POSSIBLE. THIS MAKES ITEMS SIMPLE BOTH TO FIND AND TO PUT AWAY AGAIN.

DO HAVE A DIMMER SWITCH ON THE MAIN LIGHT.

DO SEPARATE GROUPS OF ITEMS, RATHER THAN SIMPLY JUMBLING ALL TOYS OR CLOTHES TOGETHER, SO THAT IT'S EASY TO FIND WHAT'S NEEDED.

DO INDULGE YOUR CHILD'S PASSIONS WITH DISPLAY OPTIONS FOR THEIR TOYS OR OTHER COLLECTIONS.

DON'T CRAM TOO MANY FURNISHINGS IN: NARROWING ROUTES IN AND OUT OF A ROOM, OR ACROSS IT, WILL RESULT IN SOMEONE GETTING HURT AT SOME POINT.

DON'T FORGET THAT YOU CAN DESIGNATE A PLAY AREA IN ANY ROOM, NOT JUST THE CHILD'S BEDROOM.

DON'T AUTOMATICALLY USE BRIGHT COLOURS IN A CHILD'S BEDROOM; THEY CAN BE OVERSTIMULATING. WHITE OR OFF-WHITE WILL STAND THE TEST OF TIME, AND YOU CAN INTRODUCE CHARACTER THROUGH FURNISHINGS AND ACCESSORIES.

DON'T BE TEMPTED BY FLOOR- OR WALL-COVERINGS THAT ARE DIFFICULT TO CLEAN.

DON'T AUTOMATICALLY BUY 'CHILDREN'S FURNITURE'. SOLID, CLASSIC PIECES THAT CAN BE UPDATED AS THE CHILD GROWS CAN BE MUCH BETTER VALUE.

DON'T BE PESTERED INTO BUYING EXPENSIVE, FADDY ITEMS, AND IF YOU MUST BUY CHARACTER MERCHANDISE, MAKE IT SOMETHING INEXPENSIVE AND EASY TO REPLACE.

DON'T GET CARRIED AWAY WITH THE IDEA OF A MURAL: REMEMBER, YOU WILL HAVE TO PAINT OVER IT ONE DAY WHEN THE CHILD DECIDES THEY'VE GROWN OUT OF IT.

DON'T MAKE SOFT FURNISHINGS FROM FABRICS THAT AREN'T MACHINE-WASHABLE. LIFE IS TOO SHORT FOR HANDWASHING OR TRIPS TO THE DRY-CLEANER.

hallway

For many people the hall is not so much a room as a walkway between rooms, but that's not to say it's any less important. In fact, in some ways it's more so, especially if you have the kind of layout in which all rooms are accessed from a central hallway or landing: if you don't get it right, you'll be reminded every time you move from room to room.

layout

below
If your hallway is narrow, keep furniture to a minimum to avoid stubbed toes or bruised hips.

below, right
This narrow space is prevented from becoming a claustrophobic corridor because – barring a few columns – it is open-plan to the kitchen.

Whether you are blessed with the sort of hall that is a sizeable room, or have one that's more akin to a corridor, the main point to remember when it comes to what goes where is that the space must be accessible. You want to make it as easy as possible to navigate, so don't be tempted to narrow any thoroughfares with floorstanding storage. It'll be only a matter of time before someone catches themselves on it as they walk past (resulting in a bruise for them, and maybe a bit of damage to the piece, too).

colour

below
A bold combination of red, black and white is balanced by the rich tones of the parquet floor, and an eclectic collection of art.

right
Walls and woodwork in the same vivid blue, contrasted with the white floor, stairs and bench, make for a dramatic effect.

If your hallway is the common-or-garden type, without a great deal of light or square footage, avoid using dark shades on the walls, since it will make them appear to draw in even further. Of course, if you have a cavernous entrance hall, you have the option to go to town and create a grander ambience, possibly with rich tones; it'll make a great first impression on guests. Otherwise, pale shades are your friends, since they will lighten and brighten small areas. If your hall connects to stairs and a landing, consider continuing the colour scheme upstairs, to give the entire space a sense of coherence and connectedness.

Whatever the dimensions of the space, a dark floor-covering is preferable, or every speck of dirt will be immediately visible. Nobody wants to mop the floor daily, or wrestle regularly with a carpet cleaner.

walls and floors

opposite
A variety of wall-hung storage will help you keep in control of clutter without using up valuable floor space.

left
Cream carpet can be tricky in an entrance hall. If you're determined, expect it to need deep-cleaning periodically.

While carpet is luxurious, and certainly a great option if you have problems with draughts, such a high-traffic area as a hallway – with access outside – really calls for something a bit more hard-wearing and easily washable (or a very, very large doormat). If you do opt for carpet, make sure it has a suitable wear rating: something with a high proportion of natural wool is probably your best bet.

When choosing a hard floor – and tiles, timber, stone, vinyl and rubber are all suitable here – do select something that isn't slippery. Highly polished granite, for example, would be a recipe for disaster if someone with smooth-soled shoes dashed in to get out of the rain, and animals and small children could also come a cropper because of a lack of traction at the wrong moment. On a similar note, if you place rugs on a hard floor, do make sure you use some kind of anti-slip device to avoid accidents.

Walls may take a battering, too, as everything from daily schoolbags to a new bathroom suite is likely to come in at the front door and through the hall, and there's bound to be the odd scrape or splash of mud now and again. So make sure you use a paint finish that can be wiped (or, better still, scrubbed), or wallpaper that can stand up to the inevitable abuse. Another option is to protect the lower part of the wall with panelling to dado height, which is traditionally 90 centimetres.

Ceramic tiles are a hard-wearing floor option, and panelling has traditionally been used to protect hallway walls.

M ost homes are unlikely to need anything but one or two pieces of storage furniture in the hallway; indeed, in some you'd be hard pushed even to fit them in. If the passageway is wide enough, a console table or narrow cabinet can be useful, or a low stool (to make putting on shoes more comfortable), but don't worry too much if space doesn't allow anything more than the basics for storage.

opposite
Being painted the same shade as the walls, this big, roomy cupboard doesn't dominate the hallway.

left
This imposing settle is a natural fit here, not just because of its proportions, but also because it's a similar colour to the panelling behind.

below
A comfortable chair is the preferable place to perch as you put on your shoes.

storage

right
A rail is an efficient solution for lots of jackets.

below
This sleek bespoke solution allows each person their own section for shoes and coats.

opposite
Big built-in cupboards are great if there is a lot of outerwear and sports equipment to store.

Unless you're lucky enough to have a boot room or walk-in closet close to the front door, storage for coats, hats, shoes, umbrellas (etc., etc.) is going to be crucial. A nearby built-in cupboard has to be the best solution, since the inevitable jumble of items can be hidden behind a closed door. That's not to say you should let clutter take over, however. Try to make sure that everything in the cupboard has its own place, by installing shelves and shoe-racks, waterproof bags or boxes for mucky boots, and maybe a hanging pocket storage system on the back of the door for slippers, winter accessories, dog leads and other relevant accoutrements. Add a row of hooks for coats and bags, and maybe an umbrella stand, and you've got it sussed.

Without the possibility of a built-in cupboard, you have two options: wall-hung or free-standing storage. It's most likely that a combination of the two will suit best: a chest or cabinet for shoes (either specially made or simply appropriated), and wall hooks for coats and hats. A little rack or cupboard, situated out of reach of the front door, will ensure that you always know where your keys are, while somewhere to perch the day's post (or that discount coupon you simply must take with you when you go out shopping) is also a good idea.

soft furnishings

Unless you have a hallway that's more like a hotel lobby in size and function, this isn't the place for many soft furnishings, since you won't be lingering long enough to enjoy them. One notable exception, if you're having problems with draughts, is a heavy curtain hung just inside the front door (this is likely to be of most benefit in older buildings).

left
Original period doors can be draughty, so a heavily lined door curtain is sensible.

above
A wooden chair with a cushion is a comfortable place to sit when putting on your footwear.

lighting

K eep lighting simple: since you're not likely to spend a great deal of time in your hallway, you can afford to stick to functional and understated flush or semi-flush ceiling fittings, which are unlikely to get bashed as you bring in something long and unwieldy, or as that very tall friend of yours puts on his coat. Of course, if you have wonderfully high ceilings, it would be a shame not to fit a gorgeous pendant light, to make the right first impression on your visitors; just make sure it's not hanging too low or in a vulnerable position. If there's room somewhere, a lamp could be a useful addition, as, in conjunction with a timer switch, it can be a sensible security measure when you go away.

Choose the proportions of your lighting to suit your hall – and be sure to get the hanging height right.

happy home hint

IF ALL THE STORAGE YOU CAN FIT IN YOUR HALLWAY IS A ROW OF HOOKS, HANG UP AN ATTRACTIVE FABRIC SHOPPING BAG OR TWO, AND USE THEM TO STORE SUCH ACCESSORIES AS HATS, SCARVES AND GLOVES; THIS WAY THEY'RE TO HAND RIGHT NEXT TO THE COATS AND JACKETS.

accessories

right
If your front door opens directly into a living area, designate a nearby corner for coat, hat and bag storage.

far right
Your belongings, and attractive storage pieces, may be all that is needed to add a decorative touch.

below
The inside of a solid front door can make a great noticeboard, handy for times when you need to remember something on your way out.

below, right
Under-stairs cupboards are often capacious. You might want to consider fixing a peg rack inside, so that coats can be hung up out of sight.

at-a-glance guide

With the high level of traffic into and out of the house, or from room to room, this isn't the place to keep your cherished heirloom china. But a few carefully chosen (and placed) decorative items will prevent too much of a utilitarian look – unless, of course, that's what you're aiming for. Just make sure there is nothing breakable near to where people will put on their coats, and that any pictures have slimline frames and are firmly attached to the wall, so they can't get knocked off.

happy home hint

A MIRROR AND A CLOCK ARE GREAT HALLWAY ADDITIONS. ONE ENSURES YOU'LL NEVER GO OUT WITH YOUR LIPSTICK SMEARED OR TOOTHPASTE ON YOUR TOP, WHILE THE OTHER WILL (WITH LUCK) AID YOUR TIMEKEEPING.

DO TAKE INTO ACCOUNT THE DIMENSIONS OF YOUR HALL WHEN DECIDING WHETHER TO FURNISH IT WITH MORE THAN THE BASICS.

DO MAXIMIZE THE FEELING OF LIGHT AND SPACE BY CHOOSING PALE SHADES FOR THE WALLS.

DO PLAY UP THE GRANDEUR OF THE ROOM, IF IT'S SIZEABLE AND WELL PROPORTIONED.

DO EXTEND YOUR HALLWAY COLOUR SCHEME UP THE STAIRS AND INTO THE LANDING.

DO CHOOSE A DURABLE FLOOR, WHETHER HARD OR SOFT.

DO HAVE A LARGE BUILT-IN CUPBOARD FOR STORAGE, IF YOU POSSIBLY CAN.

DO INCLUDE STORAGE FOR COATS, SHOES AND HATS, AND, IF POSSIBLE, ANY OTHER BITS AND PIECES THAT NEED TO BE REMEMBERED WHEN YOU LEAVE THE HOUSE.

DO INCLUDE A LAMP WITH A TIMER SWITCH, AS A SECURITY MEASURE WHEN YOU GO AWAY.

DO ENSURE THAT ANY DECORATIVE WALL-HUNG ITEMS ARE PROPERLY SECURED.

DON'T UNDERESTIMATE HOW MUCH STORAGE YOU'LL NEED.

DON'T NARROW THE WALKWAY TOO MUCH BY SELECTING FURNITURE THAT IS TOO DEEP.

DON'T CHOOSE PALE FLOORING, OR YOU'LL SPEND A LOT OF TIME CLEANING IT.

DON'T CREATE A SLIP HAZARD WITH POLISHED TILES OR UNSECURED RUGS.

DON'T SELECT A DELICATE PAINT FINISH OR HAND-PAINTED WALLPAPER, AS THEY ARE TOO EASILY DAMAGED.

DON'T RELY ON THE CUPBOARD DOOR TO HIDE THE CLUTTER: FIT THE CUPBOARD OUT WITH SHELVES, HOOKS AND STORAGE BOXES.

DON'T FORGET THAT A HEAVY CURTAIN INSIDE THE FRONT DOOR CAN BE GREAT FOR PREVENTING DRAUGHTS (AND REDUCING YOUR HEATING BILL).

DON'T PICK A COMPLICATED OR OVERSIZED LIGHT FITTING, UNLESS THE SPACE DICTATES A MORE MAJESTIC DESIGN.

DON'T PUT FRAGILE ORNAMENTS IN THIS BUSY SPACE.

home office

holiday book

As lifestyles have altered, the old-fashioned study has been reborn as the home office. No longer a male bastion, this space can be used by any member of the household for activities that require desk space. Whether it is used for professional purposes, household administration or craft activities, it's important that this room is decorated to strike a comfortable balance between 'home' and 'workplace'.

layout

left
If more than one person is working independently in a space, try to make sure they sit facing each other.

below
You don't necessarily need a separate room for your home office; a corner of one will do.

opposite, top
Two people working on one project might prefer a large desk with chairs side by side.

Before even beginning to think about what goes where, you need to decide where your home office will be located. This could be easy – perhaps you have a dedicated room in mind – or could take a little creative thought, if space is a particularly valuable commodity in your home.

If you're creating an area for working at home in the professional sense, it should ideally be away from the busy living spaces. That way you won't be disturbed, and it will be easier for you to close the door on your work at the end of the day. It's particularly important to avoid putting a desk in your bedroom, which needs to remain a place of sanctuary to ensure a good night's sleep.

If you're planning to do your day job from home, you might even want to consider converting a loft or garage, or building a super-shed at the bottom of your garden (think what a thoroughly pleasant commute that would be). That way you can create a totally separate space that doesn't impinge on your precious time off. But if you just need a spot for household administration, consider such areas as the space under the stairs, a corner of a spare bedroom or a built-in wardrobe (which can make a great self-contained mini-office).

Once you've chosen your spot, there aren't too many layout rules to follow. Simply make sure that your chair has unimpeded access to your desk, and that frequently used objects are stored close by, and you can't go far wrong.

colour

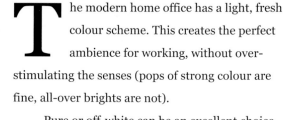

T he modern home office has a light, fresh colour scheme. This creates the perfect ambience for working, without over-stimulating the senses (pops of strong colour are fine, all-over brights are not).

Pure or off-white can be an excellent choice for walls, but do ensure that the space doesn't become clinical by adding colourful accessories, the beautiful natural tones of timber or stone, or perhaps various textures. If white isn't your thing, consider delicate shades of green, taupe or soft blue. If you can't resist a vibrant colour, why not limit it to one wall, so that it is balanced somewhat by neutral tones?

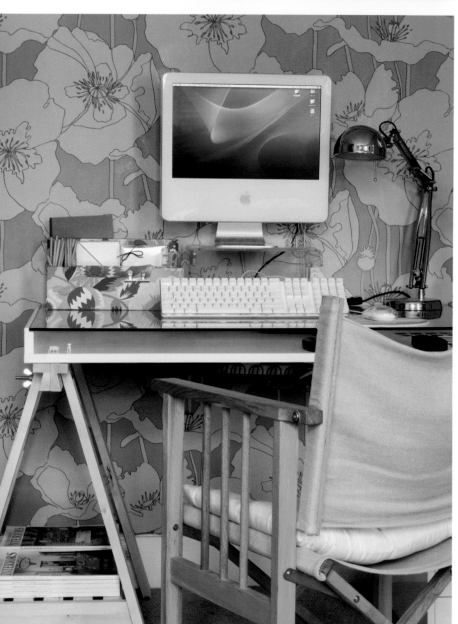

left, top
Cheerful, colourful pictures on the walls stimulate creativity and produce a positive vibe.

left
If you opt for a fabulously bold wallpaper, it's essential to keep clutter to a minimum, and choose neutral furnishings.

above
White and the natural tones of wood make for a restful environment in which to concentrate.

opposite
This palette of 1970s shades perfectly complements the retro-style desk and accessories.

walls and floors

opposite
Plain white walls, devoid of art, storage or noticeboards, can help you focus on work.

right
It's easy to spot the workspace of a creative type, with inspiring pictures and photographs, art tools and materials galore.

far right
Here, a white shelf is set against a white wall, so that the books appear to float.

below
Bare plaster isn't to everyone's taste, but here it looks great teamed with vintage office furniture.

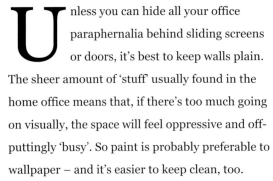

Unless you can hide all your office paraphernalia behind sliding screens or doors, it's best to keep walls plain. The sheer amount of 'stuff' usually found in the home office means that, if there's too much going on visually, the space will feel oppressive and off-puttingly 'busy'. So paint is probably preferable to wallpaper – and it's easier to keep clean, too.

A hard floor gives a slick, modern, workmanlike feel. It's particularly appropriate if your chair has castors, or if you have plans to use the space for art and craft, since it's easy to clean up after spills.

1000 on 42nd Street

happy home hint

WHY NOT INVESTIGATE
UPGRADING YOUR TECHNOLOGY?
COMPUTERS ARE NOW SMALLER
AND MORE ATTRACTIVE THAN
EVER; FLAT SCREENS TAKE UP
VERY LITTLE DESK SPACE; WHILE
WIRELESS TECHNOLOGY MEANS
YOUR ROOM WON'T BE
CLUTTERED WITH CABLES, AND
YOU'LL HAVE MORE FREEDOM IN
WHAT YOU CAN PUT WHERE.

The most critical piece of furniture in your home office is the chair. Choose one that ensures good posture, which means good lower-back support to maintain the slightly S-shaped curve of your spine. Height-wise, it should allow you to sit with your feet flat on the floor, thighs horizontal, and elbows just at desk height.

Speaking of desks, a good flat surface on which to work is essential, of course. Although they're called 'laptops', don't make the mistake of thinking that balancing a portable computer on your knee is a good option. You'll find that it overheats more easily, and you'll be more likely to drop it; it's also bad for your posture. If space is tight, choose a small writing desk, or consider a glass desk, which, being transparent, is less visually bulky.

Large desks are useful if you're running a business, or need plenty of worktop space for creative pursuits, but don't fall into the trap of getting a big office-style desk. Their proportions are often more suited to corporate spaces, and they can look awkward in a domestic setting. Besides, who wants a home office that looks like a call centre? More appealing options include a scrubbed-pine kitchen table (for those who love vintage chic), a good-sized dressing table (for a feminine look), or even a length of reclaimed timber worktop resting on sturdy metal filing cabinets (for retro revivalists).

Apart from storage – and we'll go into that in a moment – other furnishings will depend on space. A comfortable chair or two might be useful for reflective moments, and two or more chairs will be essential if you need to hold meetings, while a sofa bed is handy if you need the space to double as a spare room.

home
office

storage

happy home hint

MAKE SURE YOU BUY A LOT
MORE MAGAZINE FILES AND
STORAGE BOXES THAN YOU
THINK YOU'LL REQUIRE.
THAT WAY YOU'LL AVOID THE
PROBLEM OF YOUR CHOSEN
DESIGN HAVING BEEN
DISCONTINUED WHEN YOU
NEED TO BUY MORE.

Whatever your line of work (or your hobby), don't underestimate how much storage you will require. If your need is great, fitted shelving or cupboards will make the best use of every inch of space. Consider having sliding panels fitted to hide the clutter and create a calm, minimalist feel (this idea is also handy if your office can't be separate from your living space).

Wall shelves are another good solution: since they don't have a footprint, they can help retain a feeling of space (especially if you position them above your desk). Make sure you select the right design for your needs. Floating shelves, for example, can take only light loads; if you need something more heavy-duty for books and files, opt for the track-and-bracket type, which spreads the load. Remember to use the whole height of the wall (keep a folding step handy if need be), but reserve the top shelves for less frequently used items.

If DIY isn't your thing, place two or three freestanding shelf units along one wall. The ubiquitous white minimalist unit is great for a contemporary space, while retro fans should keep an eye out for vintage Ladderax-style shelving systems. Alternatively, seek out such pieces as kitchen dressers, wall cabinets and sideboards, which might be put to good use in an unconventional way.

Whatever type of open shelving you have, try to keep its contents easy on the eye by using well-labelled box files, jars, magazine files or storage boxes to hide the clutter. All sorts of gorgeous options are available, from vibrant block colours to pretty wallpaper designs. Or you could collect vintage tins, sewing boxes or even attractive food boxes for your own personal set of carefully mismatched storage accessories.

opposite
You can't beat a filing cabinet for keeping both work and household papers in order with the minimum of effort.

right
Open shelves allow easy access, but be careful that what you keep on them doesn't become a jumble.

far right
A small table, folding chair, noticeboard and a place to keep correspondence take up hardly any room, if carefully planned.

soft furnishings

opposite

An upholstered seat is kinder on the behind if you're sitting at your desk for any length of time.

right

If you don't work from home, and so don't spend much time at your desk, a wooden chair is fine – but you might want to add a cushion.

far right

A floor cushion, beanbag, pouffe or easy chair is a good idea for when you take a screen break.

below

If space is tight, choose a blind rather than curtains, so that your furniture can fit closer to the window.

When it comes to window dressings in the home office, blinds are a good option, since they can also be used to help regulate temperature by reflecting the sun's rays (although voiles are a softer way of achieving a similar effect). Many people prefer the sleek appearance of a blind in an office, but remember that this is also your home, so choose whatever suits your personal style.

An easy chair or comfortable sofa is a lovely addition, and great for screen breaks and creative brainstorming moments alike. Take care that you don't make this zone too comfortable, though: it is supposed to be a place of work, after all. It's far better to get your work done and dusted, then chill out in your living space, with the rest of your family.

home
office
lighting

First, if you're intending to spend a significant amount of time in your home office, you should position your desk to make best use of natural light. If you place it in front of a window, you will get the benefit without causing a glare on your computer screen, and you can take a screen break at any time simply by gazing out.

But, of course, you'll also need electric lighting – both ambient and task – for cloudy days and working late. Avoid using up valuable desk space by having a lamp that stands on the floor, is fixed to the wall, or clips to a shelf above your desk. Remember to adjust the brightness of your monitor to match the light level in the room.

opposite, top
An adjustable desk lamp is
a must for task lighting. Try
a daylight-spectrum bulb
for maximum eye comfort.

opposite, left
Positioning your desk in
front of a window avoids
screen glare, and lets you
work in lots of natural light.

opposite, bottom right
You may not be able to
gaze out of roof lights, but
they certainly help to create
a bright, airy ambience.

right
Many vintage-style desk
lamps are available, so
that you can get the look
without having to ask an
electrician to rewire your
vintage purchase.

accessories

right, top
Seek out an attractive telephone. Many retro styles are an improvement on today's less appealing models.

right
If your desk is used only occasionally, accessories can help make it less like a place of work, and more like part of the living space.

There is a lot more to a home office than a desk, chair, computer and storage: the right accessories can make all the difference. Try to look at household objects with fresh eyes. Mugs and jars make great pen pots, and you can repurpose a wall-mounted magnetic spice rack to keep rubber bands and paperclips. Or why not use a kitchen trolley as moveable storage that can be tucked away when you're not working?

A noticeboard is essential, but don't opt for brown cork; choose one of the attractive fabric-covered padded boards with criss-cross ribbons, a sheet of stainless steel with magnetic 'pins', or even a length of ribbon or string with mini pegs to keep notes handy. If you just want to be able to keep your 'to do' list visible, why not hang up a chalkboard? You could even use blackboard paint on a whole wall, to serve as both a note-taking and a doodling medium.

However carefully you choose the functional items, a few more decorative touches are always going to be needed. Intersperse books and files with ornaments and photo frames to add a personal touch, and to make things seem less office-y. The great thing about working from home is that you can alter your environment to maximize your creativity and productivity.

Finally, it may not be immediately obvious, but houseplants are a wonderful addition to the home office. They not only look cheerful, but also create a healthier environment by purifying the air. Some of the best options are the peace lily, the spider plant, the weeping fig and the bamboo palm. Just don't forget to water them!

at-a-glance guide

DO keep your workspace separate from your relaxation space.

DO consider a loft or garage conversion, or a garden retreat.

DO choose a hard floor if your chair has castors or if you're planning messy craft activities.

DO bear the proportions of the room in mind when choosing your desk.

DO include a comfortable chair for screen breaks.

DO consider a sliding door in front of fitted shelves.

DO think creatively. How can you repurpose items from other areas of the home?

DO search out attractive files, folders and boxes.

DO make the most of the natural light when planning the layout.

DO keep a number of houseplants in the room (and look after them).

DON'T set up your home office in a part of the house that is busy or noisy.

DON'T opt for a busy or very bright colour scheme, as it could be overstimulating.

DON'T compromise when it comes to choosing a comfortable and supportive chair.

DON'T buy the typical 'office furniture' you find in workplaces the world over.

DON'T underestimate how much storage you will need.

DON'T buy shelves designed for ornaments if you need to store books and folders.

DON'T place items you use all the time on very high shelves.

DON'T forget to provide task as well as ambient lighting.

DON'T buy just one or two pretty magazine files - think ahead and buy ten.

DON'T neglect to surround yourself with inspirational photographs and pictures.

outside space

Your garden (or courtyard, or balcony) isn't just outside space around your home: it's part of it, and can be a 'room' in itself. So plan it in a similarly careful way and you'll get a lot of enjoyment from it, whether you consider yourself to have green fingers or not.

layout

AVOIDING INSECTICIDES (WHICH DON'T DISTINGUISH BETWEEN HELPFUL AND HARMFUL BUGS, AND CAN BE POISONOUS TO MAMMALS, TOO) AND CHOOSING WILDLIFE-FRIENDLY PLANTS WILL NATURALLY HELP TO PREVENT GARDEN PESTS. FOR EXAMPLE, HEDGEHOGS EAT SLUGS, LADYBIRD LARVAE FEAST ON APHIDS, AND FROGS WILL HELP TO CONTROL MOSQUITO AND FLY POPULATIONS.

below
This long, narrow garden has been given better proportions through the creation of separate 'rooms', divided by flower beds.

opposite
Terraces are often used on plots with a steep incline, and can offer great views over the garden and surroundings.

The best layout for any garden, as in the case of any other part of your home, depends on the way you want to use it. A large expanse of lawn might be your idea of heaven (because it provides a big play area for your children) or of hell (because you hate mowing the grass, and tend to use the patio more). So first think about your plans for the space. The size and shape of the garden will have a significant bearing on layout, too. Long, narrow plots can have their proportions improved by being broken up into individual sections using planting and different materials, while large, flat spaces can be given more character through similar zoning.

Differing levels can be an excellent design feature. Terracing can help to make a steep slope usable as a garden, while raised beds can give structure to a smallish, square plot. However, if you have children, do keep a close eye on them, since changes of level can be a trip hazard.

Whatever the size and shape of your plot, it's worth considering the location of the different 'zones' based on their aspect. Seating areas that face north (in the northern hemisphere), for example, will always be in the shade, and so are likely to

be used less; they may even suffer problems with moss. It's most usual to position the patio or deck next to the house – preferably accessed through French doors, so that there can be an inside/outside flow – but if the back of your house is always in the shade, don't be afraid to reconsider. One convention that's worth sticking to, however, is to position the barbecue (should you wish to include one) close to the seating area, so that those in charge of the grilling can be just as sociable as everyone else.

If you enjoy growing your own produce, choose the location of your vegetable patch according to what you want to cultivate: tomatoes, peppers and squash love full sun, while broccoli, cauliflower and beets will be more than happy in part shade (indeed, crops liable to 'bolt' or go to seed, such as lettuce and spinach, are best grown away from sunny spots). Traditionally, this practical part of the garden was tucked away out of sight, but these days it's something to be proud of, rather than hide. It can be gloriously decorative as well as practical, thanks to the range of stunning varieties available (think 'Bright Lights' chard, red-leafed lettuce and bright-flowered beans growing up obelisks). There's also nothing to say that you should create a separate patch, so why not mix edibles with non-edibles? The only 'rule' worth sticking to is one of access to your herb garden: make sure that it's close to the kitchen door, so you can pinch off a bay leaf or snip some chives quickly and easily while cooking.

If you're planning a home office or a quiet studio spot, the bottom of the garden is often a good location.

colour

opposite, top
These bright-pink cushions match the flowers beautifully, while the gold-and-white masonry provides a dramatic contrast.

opposite, bottom
The palette of the English country garden is made up of myriad pretty shades, against a backdrop of lush greenery.

below
This red-painted masonry gives traditional planting a thoroughly modern twist.

happy home hint

IF YOU DON'T LIKE GETTING YOUR HANDS DIRTY BUT CAN'T AFFORD A GARDENER, WHY NOT MAKE FRIENDS WITH SOMEONE WHO'S KEEN ON GROWING THEIR OWN, BUT DOESN'T HAVE THEIR OWN PLOT? YOU COULD OFFER TO LET THEM USE PART OF YOUR GARDEN FOR THEIR FRUIT AND VEGETABLES, IN RETURN FOR KEEPING THE LAWN MOWN AND REMOVING PESKY WEEDS.

If you're planning to plant a lot of flowers, it's often a good idea to keep the backdrop neutral. Fences and walls in browns, greys or whites create a canvas against which your decorative plants can be shown off to best advantage. Bear in mind, too, the tone set by your home. You need the garden to seem at one with the building, so choose similar colours for your hard landscaping.

That said, in a very green and leafy garden a pop of bright colour can work wonders: a powder-blue shed in a cottage-style garden, perhaps, or a scattering of fuchsia and orange cushions in a tropically planted courtyard. Try taking your cue from your preferred garden theme. The Mediterranean look, for example, would have white-painted walls, blue woodwork, terracotta pots and swathes of red pelargoniums.

It's often best to restrict your floral palette unless you're very confident with colour, because it's easier to create a coherent look with fewer shades. Of course, the exceptions to that rule are meadow or cottage gardens, which use native and traditional plants respectively, and in which the many colours always seem to 'work' together.

Remember also that flowers aren't necessarily the only decorative tool in the garden. There are some lovely foliage options, including pale to dark green, silver, variegated (with flashes of white or yellow) and even reddish-leaved plants. Select your planting palette according to the character of the building: hot orange and vibrant purple blooms may suit the balcony of a contemporary white-rendered apartment block, but they risk looking brash outside a quaint old flint-built cottage.

hard landscaping

below
Gravel or stone chippings
are affordable, but can be
used only on flat surfaces.

below, right
Cobbles are available in
various types, and lend an
aged appearance to paths
and patios.

opposite, top
Here, a sleek, large-format
tile, carefully matched
to the stone furniture,
creates a minimalist,
contemporary look.

opposite, bottom
Pale paving offers a luxe
look, but it's best used in
hot, dry climates, since
algae can be a problem in
cool, wet conditions.

For coherence, choose surfaces that suit the building itself: flagstones or cobbles for period properties, perhaps, and sleek granite tiles or decking for ultra-contemporary pads. For the sake of safety, make sure that any material you use underfoot is non-slip, and if you live in a part of the world that experiences below-freezing temperatures, ensure that it's frost-proof, too. If you can use the same floor tile inside and out, or one with a very similar appearance, you'll create a continuity that will help to marry interior and exterior spaces.

If you're not fond of mowing the lawn, and your garden isn't particularly large, consider an option that is easier to look after. Gravel or slate chippings over a weed-proof membrane are largely maintenance-free, but don't take this approach for a large expanse of garden, as you'll end up with a harsh, grey wasteland. It's also a good idea to use a selection of complementary surfaces and materials, to achieve a pleasing effect. It's important to think about planting to offset the hard surfaces, but make sure the varieties you choose will survive happily with the minimum of care – and remember that planting in the ground, rather than in pots and planters, will mean fewer evenings spent watering. Alternatively, why not draw inspiration from Japanese Zen gardens, with their raked gravel and sculptural rocks? Bear in mind that no hard surface is as child-friendly as a soft lawn, so this type of low-maintenance garden isn't suitable for those with young children.

furniture

left
Vintage finds can be great in the garden, but, unless they're outdoor pieces, do put them away when it rains.

below, left
Shabby chic (even with the emphasis on the 'shabby') is a charming style for garden furniture.

below
Choose the table to suit the space: a large, rectangular table for a large, rectangular patio, for example.

opposite, top
A built-in outdoor kitchen is perfect for those who like to entertain al fresco.

opposite, bottom
This gorgeous bench is as close to sculpture as garden furniture gets.

Of course, you don't necessarily need furniture to enjoy your garden: a floor cushion or blanket laid out on the lawn may be all that's required for a spot of sunbathing. But tables and chairs of some sort are essential for al fresco meals (other than picnics), for entertaining, or if you're after more refined comfort. If the climate is warm and dry, you could create an outdoor 'living room', complete with upholstery, but otherwise it's likely that weatherproof pieces are more appropriate (unless you don't mind putting your chairs away in a shed or garage after each use).

Wood is the traditional choice, but it will need periodic repainting or oiling to keep it looking its best. Metal is also popular, although you should be careful if it's been sitting in the sun, as it can become very hot. Inexpensive plastic designs are to be avoided (they're not at all pleasant to sit on in hot weather), but some of the latest ranges of contemporary outdoor furniture are made from hard-wearing high-grade polymers that are much more comfortable and attractive.

If you're looking for the budget option, folding deck- or director's chairs are a good choice, or you could opt for a simple bench laden with comfy cushions, or even old wooden chairs and tables for a look that's laden with vintage charm. Remember, steps or low walls can act as additional seating if you're having a party, so make sure there are plenty of cushions available.

Whatever style of furniture you choose, it's a good idea to include a parasol, so that you can sit out comfortably at any time of day. Alternatively, you might want to construct your outdoor living space under a canopy, or even build a pergola and grow climbing plants up it, so that the light will be filtered by greenery.

garden buildings

right
Some designs boast two
'rooms', for those who
want their garden
buildings to serve more
than one purpose.

below
This substantial garden
building tones with the
decking and furniture.

W hether you're planning to include a shed, a summer house, a workshop, a children's play house or a home office in your garden, you need to make sure it's large enough for its purpose, but bear in mind that it also needs to be in proportion to your plot. Try not to let it dominate the space. In the small garden, a corner building can be a great choice, since it doesn't seem to encroach so much. You could also consider buying a summer house instead of a nondescript shed, as the glazing will make the building appear less bulky. If you need to control the amount of light inside, or stop people peeking in, hang blinds at the windows.

Whatever type of garden building you identify a need for, think about aspect when deciding where to place it. If you're using it as a home office, for example, you might want to have a lovely view of the garden or the landscape beyond, but if it's going to be a workshop, that won't be a consideration. Also, think about which parts of the garden get the sun; good light is particularly important for artists and makers, and can provide the feel-good factor for the home office.

Plan the inside of your shed, home office or workshop just as you would any room in your home: consider its function and include appropriate furnishings and storage. Even if you're using it simply as a place to keep gardening sundries, outdoor toys and other miscellaneous bits and pieces, you'll fit more in (and, crucially, know where to find everything) if you apply the principles of good organization.

No matter how old the shed, a lick of paint will cheerfully update it in no time.

lighting

below
Candles create an
atmospheric glow after
dark, but they must be in
lanterns so that they're not
extinguished by the breeze.

opposite
A carefully planned
lighting scheme will
enable you to make a
dramatic statement when
entertaining in the evening.

Garden lighting has three purposes: to show the garden's design off to best advantage; to create a space that's usable after dark; and to provide security. Lights for the last purpose are best attached to the house, with movement sensors positioned across approaches to the property; they can't be used for regular ambient lighting because they're on a timer.

If you want to create a comprehensive, useful lighting scheme, you'll need to have the electricity supply extended into the garden. Low-voltage systems are best, and a raft of lighting products is available. The easiest type to install doesn't actually require installation as such: solar lights don't need any wiring, and are often set on spikes pushed into the ground. They can be good for decorative effect or for marking out paths, but the illumination they give isn't strong enough to act as task lighting, even with the full charge provided by a sunny day.

Feature lighting, which is used to create additional interest, is often used to highlight statues, ponds or specimen plants, and can even be set into decking. It's also a good idea to use it to mark out paths and steps, for safety. As a temporary measure – for a party, say – you could simply use a line of tea lights in jam jars, or small lanterns, to light the way and create a pretty effect.

Ambient lighting should be provided in areas that are to be used for entertaining, especially if you're cooking outside after dark. It should not be too bright, however, and you should also bear in mind how it will affect your neighbours.

planting

below, right
'Green wall' systems are a recent innovation that is great for city courtyards; many incorporate automatic watering systems.

below
Here, a collection of mismatched pots lines a set of steps, bordered by cottage-style planting.

bottom right
If your garden gets little sun, choose such shade-loving plants as ferns and hostas.

Unless you're an experienced gardener, it's easy to feel overwhelmed when choosing plants, as there's so much choice. Making a limited selection of varieties, and having them in large numbers, will have greater visual impact than taking a pick-and-mix approach. To ensure that your chosen vegetation thrives with the minimum of intervention, you need to make

sure that the varieties you choose are right for the intended location in terms of requirements for shade or sun, damp or dry, and soil pH.

Bear in mind that perennials (which come back year after year) are an easier option than annuals (which must be planted new each year), unless the latter are self-seeding and you like the cottage-garden style. Annuals are often more colourful, though, and have more exotic-looking blooms. Whatever you choose, make sure they are planted densely but not closer than recommended for the variety, and that you encourage healthy growth through proper feeding and watering as they establish themselves. This will make it more difficult for weeds to get a look-in.

If you're not sure what will suit your garden, ask for help at your local garden centre, where the experts should have a good idea of what will thrive in your area. It's well worth doing this (or even engaging a garden designer), so that you don't waste money on plants that don't flourish, and your garden needs less care.

Speaking of effort, do consider the implications of your design when it comes to watering. If you opt for pots – and they can be a good idea, because they soften the look of hard landscaping and can add colour to even the smallest balcony – make sure you buy the largest you can, since smaller ones dry out very quickly and will need almost constant watering. Of course, one way round this is to plant cacti and succulents, which can tolerate being thirsty; just don't forget that some may need bringing indoors when there's a chill in the air. Adding water-retention gel to the soil also helps to avoid having to get the watering can out all the time. Another option is to invest in an automatic watering system of some kind, but – unless you choose the low-tech solution of a spiked water reservoire – you'll need to find a means of disguising any pipework.

at-a-glance guide

DO PLAN YOUR GARDEN ACCORDING TO ITS SIZE AND SHAPE, AS WELL AS YOUR NEEDS.

DO DIVIDE UP AWKWARDLY SHAPED OR VERY LARGE SPACES.

DO USE DIFFERENT LEVELS TO ADD INTEREST TO A BLAND SQUARE PLOT, OR TO MAKE A STEEP SLOPE USABLE.

DO CHOOSE HARD LANDSCAPING THAT SUITS THE STYLE AND MATERIALS OF YOUR HOME.

DO USE NEUTRAL SURFACE FINISHES SO THAT THE PLANTS MAKE THE IMPACT, UNLESS YOU'RE CONFIDENT ABOUT USING A POP OF COLOUR.

DO USE THE SAME FLOORING INSIDE AND OUT, IF POSSIBLE.

DO CONSIDER A LOW-MAINTENANCE GARDEN (ALTHOUGH A LAWN IS A GOOD IDEA IF YOU HAVE CHILDREN).

DO CHOOSE COMFORTABLE, HARD-WEARING FURNITURE THAT CAN EITHER LIVE OUTSIDE OR BE EASILY STORED.

DO SELECT YOUR GARDEN BUILDING ACCORDING TO THE AVAILABLE SPACE.

DO ORGANIZE YOUR GARDEN SHED, HOME OFFICE OR WORKSHOP JUST AS YOU WOULD A ROOM IN YOUR HOME.

DO PLAN THE LIGHTING AS CAREFULLY AS YOU WOULD FOR ANY OTHER PART OF YOUR PROPERTY.

DO LOOK AFTER YOUR PLANTS, SO THAT THEY GROW STRONGLY AND WEEDS CAN'T COMPETE.

DON'T FORGET THAT ASPECT IS IMPORTANT: POSITION A SEATING AREA IN THE SHADE, AND IT MIGHT NOT GET MUCH USE.

DON'T ASSUME YOUR MAIN PATIO HAS TO BE LOCATED NEXT TO THE HOUSE.

DON'T POSITION THE BARBECUE AWAY FROM THE ENTERTAINING AREA.

DON'T HIDE YOUR VEGETABLE PATCH AWAY – SHOW IT OFF.

DON'T FORGET THAT FOLIAGE CAN BE JUST AS DECORATIVE AS FLOWERS.

DON'T CHOOSE FLOOR TILES THAT AREN'T FROSTPROOF OR NON-SLIP.

DON'T ASSUME YOU HAVE TO USE SPECIALLY DESIGNED GARDEN FURNITURE: UTILITARIAN INDOOR PIECES CAN LOOK GOOD, TOO (JUST DON'T LEAVE THEM OUTSIDE).

DON'T OMIT A PARASOL OR CANOPY FROM YOUR PLANS, AS YOU'LL NEED THE SHADE ON SUNNY DAYS.

DON'T BUY CHEAP PLASTIC FURNITURE. THERE ARE PLENTY OF OTHER BUDGET OPTIONS AVAILABLE.

DON'T FORGET TO LIGHT PATHS AND STEPS, FOR SAFETY AFTER DARK.

DON'T CHOOSE PLANTS FOR THEIR APPEARANCE ALONE. THEY MUST BE SUITABLE FOR THE SPOT YOU HAVE IN MIND.

DON'T CHOOSE VARIETIES THAT NEED A LOT OF WATERING, ESPECIALLY IF THE CLIMATE IS DRY.

DON'T OPT FOR A BIG COLLECTION OF PLANTERS IF YOU'RE NOT PREPARED TO SPEND TIME WATERING.

DON'T FORGET TO ADD WATER-RETENTION GEL TO PLANTERS, POTS AND HANGING BASKETS.

one-stop

Bodie and Fou
Cool modern homewares, some with a retro edge, including furniture, lighting and accessories.
bodieandfou.com

Cox & Cox
Decorative items for the home and garden; vintage/country styling with lovely seasonal accessories.
coxandcox.co.uk

Crate & Barrel
A great one-stop with everything from beds to bowls, mostly with a contemporary vibe, although there are a few classic pieces, too.
crateandbarrel.com

Dibor
An online emporium of vintage and French-style furnishings, accessories, lighting and gifts.
dibor.co.uk

Dwell
An affordable store with modern, minimalist furniture, lighting and accessories. Particularly good for designer-inspired pieces on a budget.
dwell.co.uk

Graham and Green
Quirky, beautiful homewares with a vintage, modern, classic or humorous twist.
grahamandgreen.co.uk

Heal's
A great range of design classics by the likes of Starck and Eames, along with gorgeous contemporary furnishings, lighting, homewares and accessories.
heals.co.uk

Home Depot
Stocking everything from tiles and paint to appliances and fitted kitchens, this DIY store has branches all over the United States.
homedepot.com

IKEA
Bringing Scandinavian style to the world, this home-furnishings giant is particularly good for inexpensive yet stylish furniture and fun, colourful accessories.
ikea.com

John Lewis
A British institution, this store offers high-quality homewares from a variety of well-known brands. 'Never knowingly undersold.'
johnlewis.com

Laura Ashley
Classic country looks. Particularly good for stylish upholstery and pretty decorative accessories.
lauraashley.com

Lombok
Handcrafted furniture with an Eastern influence, great for creating an exotic feel with a touch of traditional colonial.
lombok.co.uk

Notonthehighstreet.com
Check out the home and garden section; designer-makers sell through this site, so the choice of decorative accessories and artwork is particularly good.
notonthehighstreet.com

OKA
Classic furniture and accessories with a contemporary edge. Influences include French country, Charles Rennie Mackintosh, oriental and Swedish style.
okadirect.com

Pale & Interesting
Vintage chic, including antique furniture and pieces made from reclaimed materials. Some lovely classic household linens, and a beautiful range of simple glassware.
paleandinteresting.com

Pottery Barn
Elegant furnishings for every room in the house, and outdoors, too. Great selection of vintage-looking pieces, as well as more polished styles.
potterybarn.com

Rockett St George
Funky pieces that ooze individuality, including great lighting, vintage furniture and artwork.
rockettstgeorge.co.uk

Rose & Grey
Quirky homewares with a vintage/retro edge, particularly good for kids' rooms: check out the fabulous range of wall stickers.
roseandgrey.co.uk

paint and wallpaper

AURO
Eco paints made from natural and organic materials, with formulae for interior and exterior woodwork as well as interior walls.
auro.co.uk

Beckers
A Swedish paint brand that offers an infinite range of colours: match any shade exactly and choose from a range of finishes for floors, walls and woodwork, for both inside and out.
beckerspaints.co.uk

Craig & Rose
Eggshell, matt, metallic, satin, suede, pearlized and glitter finishes in a wide range of colours, but particularly good for its palette of historic shades.
craigandrose.com

Farrow & Ball
Traditional wallpapers and paints with a period feel. Wonderful range of colours, including a famously large selection of whites.
farrow-ball.com

Fired Earth
Eggshell and matt emulsion in a variety of beautiful shades, including ranges based on mid-twentieth-century fashions and the decor at National Trust properties.
firedearth.com

Graham & Brown
Wallpaper galore, from quirky and colourful geometric designs to traditional damasks, and from Celtic-inspired designs to chinoiserie. Also offers wall art and paint.
grahambrown.com

Little Greene
Beautiful wallpaper and paint, especially good for twentieth-century style aficionados, with a range of 1950s wallpaper, and paints for achieving the look of the '30s, '50s, '60s and '70s.
littlegreene.com

Morris & Co
Wallpaper from this historic manufacturer of authentic Arts and Crafts designs represents traditional English style at its best. There's a range of matching fabrics, too.
william-morris.co.uk

Sanderson
Classic wallpaper, from English chintzes to graphic 1950s designs, via stylized florals, toiles and textured plains.
sanderson-uk.com

Secondhand Rose
A gem of a vintage wallpaper shop, based in New York City. Original papers for bathrooms, kitchens and kids' rooms, as well as florals, geometrics and damasks, and a selection of faux finishes.
secondhandrose.com

flooring

Alternative Flooring
Gorgeous wool carpets as well as a wide range of natural-fibre options, including coir, sisal, jute and seagrass.
alternativeflooring.com

Amtico
Hard-wearing floor-coverings for all areas of the home, including faux stone and timber finishes, as well as colourful options.
amtico.com

BCA Antique Materials
French architectural salvage and building materials, including floorboards, chimneypieces, stone flooring and reclaimed tiles.
bca-antiquematerials.com

Brintons
Carpets and runners in a wide selection of plain and patterned styles, including the popular Laura Ashley range.
brintons.net

Craven Dunnill
Ceramic tiles for walls and floors, from traditional designs to contemporary surfaces. Also a good selection of natural stone, and some stunning mosaic options in metal and glass.
cravendunnill.co.uk

Crucial Trading
Rugs and floor-coverings made from natural fibres, including wool, coir, jute, sisal and seagrass.
crucial-trading.com

Dalsouple
Funky flooring made from natural or synthetic rubber, in a variety of colours and patterns, with a smooth or textured finish.
dalsouple.com

Ebony and Co
Handcrafted solid wood floors, from the palest American white ash to the darkest wenge.
ebonyandco.com

Harvey Maria
A wide selection of vinyl floor tiles, including stone and timber effects, as well as quirky options, such as photographic finishes, and a Cath Kidston range.
harveymaria.co.uk

Johnson Tiles
A huge collection of wall and floor tiles, including ceramic, stone, glass, porcelain and marble, plus a range of Victorian-style designs for fireplaces.
johnson-tiles.com

Junckers
Solid and engineered wooden flooring, available as strip or wide boards, in natural timber finishes and colourful stained options.
junckers.com

Kersaint Cobb & Company
Beautiful rugs and carpets in natural fibres, including wool, mountain grass, sisal and jute, plus a range of timber flooring.
kersaintcobb.co.uk

Reed Harris
Tiles for walls and floors, inside and out, with a particularly striking collection that's great for feature walls.
reedharris.co.uk

Roger Oates Design
Runners, rugs, fabrics and accessories all available in this designer's trademark stripes.
rogeroates.com

furniture

And So to Bed
Handmade beds, plus bedroom furniture and fine linen, all inspired by period style. A raft of gorgeous designs ranging from a simple metal bedstead to an ornate sleigh with gold-leaf finish.
andsotobed.co.uk

Demosmobilia
With originals dating from the 1930s to the 1980s, this vintage-furniture emporium stocks only the highest-quality designer pieces.
demosmobilia.ch

Gautier
A French furniture brand specializing in sleek contemporary designs. Particularly good for clean-lined storage furniture.
gautier.fr

Grange
Classic French chic. Elegant furniture, including dining tables and chairs, cabinetry, coffee tables and modular storage units.
grange.fr

The Holding Company
Storage options galore, from little boxes for bits and pieces to chests and modular shelf systems.
theholdingcompany.co.uk

Lassco
High-end architectural salvage, reclaimed materials and antiques. Packed to the rafters with stunning pieces and curiosities.
lassco.co.uk

Leporello
Painted furniture in classic and contemporary styles. French and Swedish style influences are apparent.
leporello.co.uk

Ligne Roset
Designer furnishings for contemporary living, with cutting-edge style for living rooms, dining rooms, home offices and bedrooms.
ligneroset.com

The Old Cinema
A wonderful range of antique, vintage and retro pieces, including eye-catching upcycled furnishings.
theoldcinema.co.uk

Roche Bobois
Achingly hip furniture for every room in the house, as well as outdoor pieces, plus a range of elegant decorative accessories.
roche-bobois.com

Scumble Goosie
Buy ready-to-paint furniture blanks in French and Gustavian styles and put your own stamp on them, or buy ready-finished for instant impact on your interiors.
scumblegoosie.co.uk

Sweetpea & Willow
A lovely selection of French furniture, from rustic to ornate styles with gold embellishment.
sweetpeaandwillow.com

fabrics and soft furnishings

Anta Scotland
Gorgeous tartans in worsted wool and linen, plus woollen tweed and a range of throws, cushions and other home accessories.
anta.co.uk

Cabbages & Roses
Vintage-style florals, plus retro stripes and checks, as well as a lovely Toile de Jouy.
cabbagesandroses.com

Cath Kidston
A charming and cheerful selection of vintage-inspired prints, including brilliant options for children and a range of pretty-yet-practical oilcloth.
cathkidston.co.uk

Celia Birtwell
A collection of wonderful illustrative prints, many of which have a retro air.
celiabirtwell.com

Designers Guild
Striking collections of prints and plains in jewel-like colours, as well as more restrained palettes. Lovely options for children's rooms.
designersguild.com

Elanbach
Vintage-style printed linens and cottons, including florals and stripes, as well as oriental designs and paisley.
elanbach.com

Gingerlily
Silk-filled duvets, mattress toppers and pillows, along with silk bedlinen and blankets.
gingerlily.co.uk

Ian Mankin
Plains, patterns and checks in cotton and linen, plus the biggest collection of stripes you could wish for.
ianmankin.co.uk

Kate Forman Fabrics
Plain and patterned linen and a sumptuous range of velvets, all in a pretty, restrained palette of soft pinks, blues, greens and golds.
kateforman.co.uk

Lewis & Wood
Great for large-scale prints, particularly of quirkier subjects for fabric, including fish and horses. Also offers matching wallpaper.
lewisandwood.co.uk

Peacock Blue Home
Simply gorgeous soft furnishings, including bedlinen, throws, quilts and cushions.
peacockbluehome.co.uk

Prêt à Vivre
Choose from a huge range of fabrics, and have a variety of curtains and blinds made to measure.
pretavivre.com

Urban Burp
A fantastic selection of vintage fabrics, including some rarities, plus a great choice of reproductions. Arts and Crafts to mid-century modern and beyond.
urbanburp.com

Vanessa Arbuthnott
Printed linen and cotton fabrics, with nature-inspired illustrative motifs; also wallpaper, rugs and furniture.
vanessaarbuthnottfabrics.co.uk

The White Company
Plain and pretty (white) bedlinen, cushions and throws, as well as towels, nightwear and other home accessories.
thewhitecompany.com

lighting

Bella Figura
A huge range of designer lighting, from sleek Art Deco wall lights to ornate Venetian glass chandeliers.
bella-figura.com

Christopher Wray
Stunning lighting designs, from authentic period style to cutting-edge contemporary.
christopherwray.com

The French House
Pendants and wall lamps for indoors and outdoors, all with a vintage appeal.
thefrenchhouse.net

Holloways of Ludlow
A great selection of ceramic rise-and-fall pendants, prismatic shades and industrial-style lighting. Definitely one for those who favour vintage/retro style.
hollowaysofludlow.com

Jim Lawrence
Lighting made in forged iron or solid brass, with some fantastic period styles. Also available is a classic range of lampshades.
jim-lawrence.co.uk

John Cullen Lighting
Specialists who not only stock an immense range of styles, but also offer a design service for lighting schemes.
johncullenlighting.co.uk

SKK Lighting
Great modern designs. Particularly good for fun lamps in the shape of various animals.
skk.net

The Wooden Lamp Company
Cute table lamps with turned wooden bases painted in cheerful colours, topped with funky fabric shades.
thewoodenlampcompany.co.uk

accessories

Bombay Duck
Quirky and fun homewares, with styles varying from simple chic to kitsch. Check out the selection of cupboard and door knobs, great for glamming up plain furnishings.
bombayduck.co.uk

Cloudberry Living
Scandinavian home accessories, including pieces in traditional and contemporary styles, from a variety of designer brands.
cloudberryliving.co.uk

The Contemporary Home
Huge range of good-value pieces for every room of the home, from everyday essentials to fun bits and bobs.
tch.net

Cucina Direct
Shopping heaven for the keen cook: everything from cake tins to kitchen electricals.
cucinadirect.com

Emma Bridgewater
Glorious hand-painted earthenware in a variety of designs, plus accompanying ranges of melamine, glassware, tins and cutlery.
emmabridgewater.co.uk

Greengate
Cheerful vintage-style homewares, including stoneware, melamine, kitchen textiles, cushions and throws.
greengate.dk

Hunkydory Home
Handmade cushions and lampshades in a range of funky designs, plus clocks, tableware, tea towels, wall art and other goodies.
hunkydoryhome.co.uk

Willow & Stone
A bit like an old-fashioned hardware store, with a wealth of gorgeous period-style door furniture and ironmongery, as well as all sorts of lovely vintage accessories.
willowandstone.co.uk

b = bottom; t = top; l = left; r = right

Graham Atkins-Hughes: 36b, 65bl, 140, 148bl, 154tr, 155, 178br, 179b; Devis Bionaz: 19r, 55l, 69b, 77b, 78t, 128t, 131t; Johnny Bouchier: 30r, 50b, 52b, 58–59b, 174b; Nick Carter: 19l, 29b, 56t, 62, 74, 76b, 78b, 81t, 96t, b, 113, 129, 146l, 162 (Swedish Interior Design, swedishinteriordesign.co.uk), 163b, 164br, 184l; Bieke Claessens: jacket back tr, 2–3, 66b, 86t (decoration: Annemie & Stefaan de Ceuleneer), 88, 95, 97, 138r, 144b (architect: Bart Lens); David Cleveland (styling: Milly Goodwin): 20l, 154b; Nikki Crisp: 182; Dan Duchars: jacket front, jacket back b, 7b, 20tl, 24–25, 29t, 46, 58t, 63t, 64t, 66t, 70–71, 105b, 114, 115b, 125, 132tl, 134l, r, 157bl, 165, 166t; Donna Eaves: 39r; Sara Essex: 91; Emotive Images: 51t, 184br; Cristina Fiorentina: 153b; Jake Fitzjones: jacket back c, 6, 12, 20tr, 22l, 42, 48r, 65t, 72b, 92bl, 103, 105t, 108t, 110, 118–19, 128b, 132b, 152; Douglas Gibb: 26t, b, 32–33, 35, 36t, 47b, 63bl, 68l, 89b, 98–99, 101t, b, 116–117b, 120, 131b, 146r, 160, 172–73, 176l; Tria Giovan: 18, 43t, 87, 92t, 100, 109, 121, 142r–143l, 145, 157t, 177b; Bruce Hemming: 77t, 86b; House & Leisure: 10–11 (/J. de Villiers/ GAP/Inside), 14t (/D. Ross), 14b (/M. Hall; architect: Pieter Malan), 15t (/Elsa Young; styling: Leana Schoeman), 16–17 (styling: Tracey Lee Lynch), 22r (/Mark Williams; styling: Jeanne Botes), 28t (styling: Tracey Lee Lynch), 31 (/Mark Williams; designer: Kate Moffrat), 34 (/Elsa Young; styling: Leana Schoeman), 37 (/Greg Cox; styling: Retha Erichsen), 38 (/D. Chatz), 44–45 (/D. Chatz), 55r (styling: Lisa Adams), 64bl (/W. Heath), 64br (/D. Chatz), 67 (/D. Chatz/zululand@global.co.za), 76t (/D. Chatz), 80t (/J. de Villiers), 80–81b (/S. Chance; architect: M. Pennington),

104 (/D. Chatz), 112t (/M. Hoyle; architect: W. Wilsenach), 115t (/P. Baasch), 116t (styling: Tracey Lee Lynch), 117t (styling: Julia Stadler), 123l (styling: Julia Stadler), 123r (/S. Calitz), 127b (/Elsa Young; styling: Sherri Chipps), 139l (/Patrick Toselli; styling: Leigh Toselli), 141t (/Mark Williams), 149 (/D. Chatz), 154tl (/J. de Villiers), 166b (/Elsa Young; styling: Leana Schoeman), 168–69 (/J. de Villiers), 175 (/P. Gordon; designer: Kamstra & Holmes), 178bl (/J. de Villiers); Alexander James: 13, 60–61, 170, 184tr (architect: Chris Dyson); Patric Johansson: 144t; Nick Keane: 39l; Bill Kingston: 9, 53, 93r, 106b, 142l (design: bombarock.co.uk); Julia Klimi: 177t; Guillaume de Laubier: 112b; Nadia Mackenzie: 43b, 93l, 94b, 156, 180b; Alistair Nicholls: 179t; Clive Nichols: 139r (walls: Farrow & Ball Down Pipe No. 26; floor and stairs: F&B Slipper Satin No. 2204), 183 (/Charlotte Rowe); Mark Nicholson: 52b, 141b; Lizzie Orme: 92br, 111; Yvonne Oswald: 136–37; Richard Parsons: 72t; Costas Picadas: 27, 48l, 50t, 51b, 54r, 56b, 57, 73, 75, 90t, 102l, 122, 126, 127t, 132tr, 143r, 147, 148tl, 158, 161l, 164t, l, 171, 176r, 178t; Spike Powell: 85, 107b; Maayke de Ridder: 47t; James Robinson: 79, 89t; Mark Scott: jacket back tl, 7t, 21, 30l, 40, 41, 54l, 102r, 106t, 124, 130, 138l, 157br, 163tl, tr, 181; Rachael Smith: 59t, 63br, 65b, 84, 107t; Warren Smith: 94t; Chris Tubbs: 49 (designer: Charles Mellersh); Amanda Turner: 15b, 108b, 180t; Rachel Whiting: 28b, 68r, 82–83, 90b, 133, 148br, 150–51, 153t, 159; Christina Wilson: 69t, 174t

index

First published 2012 by Merrell Publishers,
London and New York

Merrell Publishers Limited
81 Southwark Street
London SE1 0HX

merrellpublishers.com

British Library Cataloguing-in-Publication data:
Winward, Rebecca.
Happy home.
1. Interior decoration. 2. Interior
decoration–Psychological aspects.
I. Title
747-dc23

ISBN 978-1-8589-4571-2

Produced by Merrell Publishers Limited
Designed by Alexandre Coco
Project-managed by Rosanna Lewis
Indexed by Hilary Bird

Printed and bound in China

Acknowledgements

I'd like to thank my lovely husband, Matt, for all his
support (and cups of tea). I'm also grateful to the
wonderful team at Merrell for giving me the chance to
bring *Happy Home* into being, and would like to thank
them for all their hard work in creating such a beautiful
book. Additionally, I'd like to thank GAP Interiors for
supplying such fantastic images of happy homes the world
over, and of course thanks must also go to the design-
savvy owners of those homes, without whose expertise
we would not have been able to illustrate this book in
such an inspirational way.